I.
Intuitional
Intelligence

How the Awareness of Instinctual Gut Feelings Fosters Human Learning, Intuition, and Longevity

Martha Char Love
And
Robert W. Sterling

We dedicate this book to the awareness of Human Gut Instincts and the path to higher Intuitional Intelligence.

We often forget that there is an inner direction of the Human Being that has far greater chance to successfully develop and function than anything we could superimpose upon the person.

TABLE OF CONTENTS

Introduction

Increasing Intuitional Intelligence: How the Awareness of Instinctual Gut Feelings Fosters Human Learning, Intuition, and Longevity is written as a companion to our book published in 2011, *What's Behind Your Belly Button? A Psychological Perspective of the Intelligence of Human Nature and Gut Instinct.* It is a response to the readers who have asked us to share more on how our knowledge of uniting Human multiple brains—gut and head—affects current theory and practice in a number of subject areas as well as life experience, wellness, and the evolution of mind.

We have selected the title *Increasing Intuitional Intelligence* because the ultimate goal of our lives' work has been to increase human intelligence through the development of our intuition. You may have already learned from business coaches that intuition is used for a majority of important decisions by the most successful business executives. They will often say that all we have to do is to listen to our intuition and act on it to develop it further. While it is true that it is important to practice using our intuition, there is a part of the learning process of developing intuition that we can not skip, and that is the inner work part. We can not skip right to the enlightenment state and be intuitively intelligent without quite a bit of inner work and self-awareness. That is what this book and *What's Behind Your Belly Button?* is all about—the inner work it takes to become aware of your instinctual gut feelings to unite the gut and head brains and to increase Intuitional Intelligence.

First we must take the time to clear the emotional channels within us, clear out our old ways of perceiving ourselves and accompanying emotions that are blocking our intuitive awareness. This is where freeing our instincts and listening to our gut feelings is essential. Our Intuitional Intelligence connects instinct and feeling (our unconscious) with reason and sensory input (our conscious mind) and is brought forward in our awareness as insight. Intuitional Intelligence is linked to our awareness of our Human Nature and the ability to be aware of our unconscious—our own inner state of being (self-awareness)—and to being aware of the feeling state of others (empathy). It makes sense even to the logical mind that the first place to begin our work to increase our Intuitional Intelligence is within our own instinctual feeling state, where the impact of life is registered in our gut feelings of emptiness and fullness.

The problem has been that most people in our modern world are not aware of the important role of the gut holding our feeling memory and registering how life is impacting us. Our feelings of emptiness and fullness that is felt in our guts and relate to how well our needs as human beings are being met have for so long been confused in our awareness with the feelings of emptiness and fullness that accompanies hunger. We have missed the awareness of this vital feeling gauge in our gut. Until this feeling awareness in the gut is recognized and time is spent becoming aware of our gut feelings and the impact of life upon us from early childhood, we can not step forward in developing higher mind and Intuitional Intelligence.

In this book we will look further at the process of education of our instincts and lay the foundations for evolving higher mind

2

and creative thinking. We talk quite a bit about the education of the young because we think that the learning process about the instinctual gut feelings we are born with begins at birth and needs to be included in the educational program as early as preschool age. In time, with proper care and attention, education, and a culture that supports instinctual awareness, the child will learn more and more to be attuned to his/her instincts. As his/her logical brain develops along with the awareness of his/her instincts and gut feelings, the child develops Intuitional Intelligence and a higher creative mind.

You will find *Increasing Intuitional Intelligence* is divided into five main units that include essays on the affects of consciousness of our gut instincts on many areas of life experience and are as follows: 1. Step One to Increasing Intuitional Intelligence! Educating the Gut Brain, Learning, Gut Feeling Awareness, & Childhood Development; 2. Instinctual Awareness and Its Affects Upon Longevity; 3. Gut Feelings and Intuitional Intelligence as Applied to Psychology 4. How the Consciousness of the Gut as a Brain Affects Religion and Culture; and 5. How Uniting our Multiple Brains Affects Health and Wellness and the Medical Profession.

Within these essays, we address a variety of subject areas exploring the importance of gut instincts and using gut intelligence in: the aging process (beginning at birth), emotions, developing Intuitional Intelligence, longevity, happiness, memory, fear of death and dying, decision-making, inner human needs, the learning process, children and school, parenting, social bonds, marriage, body awareness, personality development, emotional intelligence, relationships, human communications and technology, creativity, evolution of mind and our relationship to spiritual beliefs and religion, cultural history, and the medical profession.

In *What's Behind Your Belly Button?*, we turned the current behavioral understanding of the Human psyche held in popular academia upside-down, inside-out and bottom-up with our conclusions from our clinical research based on our 40+ years of counseling and educational experiences that explored how people use their gut feeling responses as a source of intelligence. We demonstrated the idea of a two-brain system of intelligence—gut and head—in the Human being. In *Increasing Intuitional Intelligence,* we explain just how the two brain system functions psychologically for positive growth and development, well-being, a fulfilled life, and ultimately for developing our higher mind or Intuitional Intelligence.

We realize that this material is not easy to fully comprehend because it is both academic (requiring the use of the thinking brain) and also readers must research their own inner feelings (requiring the use of the feeling gut brain) and experiences to make sense of the new psychological image (view) of Human Nature that we propose. Most of us have very little experience with the conscious awareness of our gut feelings, so this is new to most people. We have found that readers and researchers alike are fascinated with the subject and have many questions about living with gut instincts and making the most of gut intelligence.

Although it is new for most of us to think of ourselves as having multiple brains as intelligence sources, it is an exciting prospect that hits home with many people even as they first begin to read about it and consider it in their own experience of themselves. To first become aware that you have a gut brain that has been guiding your behavior toward fulfilling your inner instinctive Human needs, explains much about ourselves and why we do and feel what we do. As a result, we have had many enthusiastic readers write to us, tell us they are successfully using the complete protocol for the Somatic Reflection Process that we include in *What's Behind Your Belly Button?* for exploring gut feelings, and then ask us questions about how to further use gut feelings to unite the thinking and feeling brains to achieve well-being and happiness with a variety of life circumstances and issues. It is to answer many of these questions that we have written this second book, *Increasing Intuitional Intelligence.*

It is our hope that *Increasing Intuitional Intelligence* will help take our theories and interpretations of Human gut instincts into a place in current scientific knowledge that will revolutionize Behavioral Science and include a more functional model of the Human being. By a more "functional" model, we mean a way of thinking of who we are that is actually "usable" and "workable" when applied to Human life and allows for successful and happy living.

While gaining much attention to those interested in exploring gut intelligence, our clinical findings still lack substantial peer research and review. Our theories on Human instincts and gut intelligence are just now on the cusp of edging into a place in mainstream popular psychology and medicine with many research studies now being conducted on the importance of the gut brain and its affects upon mental health. For instance, recent Medical studies on mice headed by Premysel Bercik at Farncombe Family Digestive Health Research Institute at McMaster University show that neonatal stress in early life, such as maternal separation, changes the newborn's gut bacteria and leaves it vulnerable to a variety of disorders that include disturbing gut functioning and interrupting the proper

5

functioning of the head brain. This has been found to lead to anxiety and depression in adult life. Anxiety and Depression Association of America have calculated that Anxiety Disorders affects 40 million adults. These recent findings on the affects of early life stress on gut flora that lead to our most prominent disorder in Mental Health today are propelling research toward exploring the importance of somatic techniques (like the Somatic Reflection Process that we developed) to reduce stress levels and heal wounds of separation and anxiety.

The concepts of gut intelligence that we put forward are based upon our clinical experiences and what we have learned from the reported affects of using the Somatic Reflection Process that we developed on gut feeling awareness with hundreds of people, including ourselves. So while much of what we write may seem like conjecture and assumption, it is based on ample professional clinical experience. Our experience makes it very difficult for us to be quiet, even if our theories fly in the face of traditional academia. We are hoping that our discussions in this book will influence neurologists and other medical scientists, psychologists, educators, and graduate students in a variety of areas of study to conduct further research and experiments using our protocol of the Somatic Reflection Process to render more hard data on the affects on Human life of being more conscious of our gut feelings and instincts and uniting the two centers of intelligence.

Of course, the idea of the gut as a center of intelligence relating to Intuitional Intelligence is not new. For instance, the ancient Hindu placed the astral soul of Humans (one's self-consciousness) in the pit of the stomach. For the modern Parsis (see *Isis Unveiled* and translation from the *Vedic* Sanskrit hymn in Rig-vedas) there exists a belief up to the present time that

6

spiritual adepts have a flame in their navel that enlightens them and shows them the spiritual world and all things unseen, even at a distance. They call this inner vision through the gut the Lamp of Deshtur. And while a number of Mesolithic cultures revered the gut as a main center of intelligence, we propose that we have never had a culture with a balanced integration of the head and gut brains. In fact, modern people in general have left behind the consciousness of the belly and marginalized the importance of the enteric nervous system as a center of intelligence in favor of the upper thinking brain. Without the awareness of the gut brain information in our thinking, we leave out perhaps the greatest piece of information needed in our perception to help us make sound judgments through our intuition—and that is "the impact of life upon us from moment-to moment". Now our task is to unify the two brains.

In our first book, *What's Behind Your Belly Button?,* we have proposed a protocol and demonstrated the Somatic Reflection Process that we created in the 70s and used with people in counseling to do just that—unify the two brains. And by using this process with individuals, one person at a time, we can bring back the awareness of our gut responses so that we can unify our gut and head brains, thus developing a clear circuit of information in our perception to give rise to our Intuitional Intelligence. We see the increase of Intuitive Intelligence as an inevitable step for our human species if we are to survive and it will make many things possible that have only so far been speculated in science fiction or esoteric philosophical texts. Of course, these changes will only come through our need for adaption and survival. But as you will see as you read this book, the pressure to do so is already at our doorstep.

The subject of gut feeling intelligence as a path to developing Intuitional Intelligence is so new to our modern world that there is a great need for ample clarification of its meaning so that people may begin to understand within their own experience of themselves what these gut feelings are all about. This clarification also allows for the development of a model of Human Nature that is functional and successful in building a happy and peaceful world.

It is important to both feel into our gut feelings in the body and then to also understand with our thinking brain just what we are feeling, how our gut feelings are organized to reflect Human need, and what it means to have a Human Nature. We are not advocating the elimination of the use of the thinking brain in favor of a swing toward the use of the gut brain, but for the uniting of these two brains into a more functional Human intelligence system than ever before in Human history. It is only with these two brains working in unity— integrating our conscious and subconscious processes—that we can as a species, through time, develop our Intuitional Intelligence and evolve higher mind from our inner vision. Are we ready and able to make this needed advance in intelligence? We think so!

Part 1

Step One to Increasing Intuitional Intelligence! Educating the Gut Brain, Learning, Gut Feeling Awareness, and Childhood Development

Freeing Human Nature: The Process of Human Learning and the Two Brain System—Head and Gut

You may have picked this book up to read because you would like to increase your Intuitional Intelligence. Step One in doing so is to understand and educate the two brain system. It takes both the head and gut brain working as a unity to reach the goal of developing Intuitional Intelligence. This is not a quick process but one you will benefit from every step of the way.

The following is a unique discussion about our work as counselors and educators exploring gut feelings and it includes a philosophy of science based upon our research findings. While it is a profound description and definition of the Human two brain system, it will certainly raise both questions and answers in the field of education and learning concerning the importance of educating both our head and gut brains, as well as what that means for our future culture and development as a species as we free Human Nature and Natural Law.

Human Nature requires a learning process that is free to utilize all of the brains with which it is born. The intelligence within the ancient animal brain has developed its knowledge over millions of years of experience to plan, build and improve the quality of life it represents. This brain manages its functional duties with the enteric nervous system in the gut, and 'speaks' with its feeling instincts. And then there is the other center of intelligence, which grows after birth as the sensory brain. The sensory brain develops the sense of sight, sound, taste, touch, and smell over time. It is focused on the world outside the gut and it expresses itself with the voice of its environments in the outside world. It is what we often refer to as the thinking brain.

For many centuries educators have focused on the sensory brain as the main center of functional intelligence and have reported it as the center to be educated. Some of us are beginning to realize that by focusing on the senses and trying primarily to educate the thinking brain about the outside world, we have omitted many positive qualities of knowledge that each of us need or will need in life.

There has been a fairly recent shift of interest to the two brain system of education. This was initiated in education by community college behavioral science classes and exploration groups in self-awareness in the 70s. Over two decades later, medical research discovered and validated the presence of two independent centers of intelligence, both essential to learning. These centers of learning represent two separate independent brains. This awareness has radically changed our Human functional image from a single brain system to a multiple brain system, with both an externally focused sensory brain and an internally focused animal brain.

The current growing awareness of the presence of the two brains is not a discovery that such brains existed, for their existence has been long known and associated with the intelligence necessary for the design and production of the

Human instincts at birth. However, this recent neurological exploration of the two independent brains provides science with a better understanding of the internal and external functions of the life process, how the systems work, and what they can do for the learning process of the Human animal.

Exploring the Intelligence of the Gut in Education

We are going to backtrack a little here and explain briefly our own history of exploring the gut brain in an educational setting. In 1975, we had discovered (with hundreds of people we were working with in counseling) a response in the gut that appeared to isolate a feeling aspect separate from the sensory brain. This gut response seemed to be pure feelings of emptiness or fullness (not to be confused with hunger or lack of hunger) without a thinking or sensory component. We were operating a career guidance center and coaching/facilitating Behavioral Science classes at the time. We were using a technique we developed of somatically reflecting upon the gut feelings a person was having in the present around a troublesome issue, then going back through time with the awareness of that feeling. Using this process, we assisted students in finding any disturbing experience of the past that was interfering with present self-awareness and might affect future employment stability.

Having found that most students experienced past traumas, we would have the students bring together their thinking and feeling—two points of view—of what he or she discovered about themselves in somatic reflection. This technique would

13

generally remove the stress from their life. When they had finished their inner reflection, we would have them move back to the present time awareness, carefully watching for the feeling of the original disturbance to see how it had woven its influence all the way to the present. This technique is now known as, the Somatic Reflection Process (SRP). We refer you to our book *What's Behind Your Belly Button?* for a complete protocol and verbatim examples of counseling sessions.

The minds of medical practitioners have long wrestled with the understanding of what goes on between the throat and the anus. But the truth about the enteric nervous system had to wait for certain internal tools, minds, and materials of discovery. In 1998 Dr. Michael D. Gershon published the results of his medical research discoveries on the intelligence of the enteric nervous system in his book, *The Second Brain: A ground breaking new understanding of nervous disorders of the stomach and intestine*. It was our goal to take what was a complex Human system—the enteric nervous system—and transpose what we understood from Gershon's new medical perspective into a psychological perspective that was based on our understanding of gut feeling intelligence. This move validated our own experience with exploring gut feelings in counseling in the 70s. And now that we had a growing awareness of intelligence concerning the Human gut, we realized that it was wise to utilize at least some of our energy toward learning how to manage that intelligence in making more healthy choices in individual lives.

The Human Story Begins with Instinctual Intelligence

Individuality is a key word when describing Human Nature. A quick review of the Human story reveals that we begin at conception, each of us with a unique set of genes. Within that set are portions, sub-sets, which define different aspects of the organism. A portion of the genes is set aside to prepare the electrochemical materials to form a zygote, and a portion of the genes prepares the 'ground work' for a recognizable Human Being at birth time.

Immediately after birth is the time when we can see how important the instincts are to the learning process, both to the mother and to the newborn. Mother 'sets the table' instinctively, and the newborn 'pulls up a chair', and without any external instruction begins to exercise its instinctual intelligence—hunger to stay alive. Midwives will tell you that since babies take all their nutrition from the mother in the womb, it is the unusual baby that needs no coaxing to nurse immediately upon birth. Most babies are not really hungry until a few hours after birth. After continued exposure to the mother's breast and hunger sets in, the instinctive intelligence of the baby to suckle will begin the nursing process. Our instinctual intelligence is passed along to each of us, with slight modifications, from our inherited gene pool. The individual— what we learn and how we learn about our selves—and the outside world are the result of the environmental impact in which we were born and raised. It should be quite obvious that the instincts of the animal brain are essential to the beginning of Human life. Experience with the gut intelligence of the animal brain is essential to the learning process and to the satisfactions of the animal species as long as that organism is alive.

The evidence of essential need for the instincts in the animal brain and its enteric nervous system (ENS) is its important functionality associated with the life processes in the entire body. After all, the ENS is the result of the DNA plan and the construction of that plan, which was conceived by the genetic inheritance it was offered. Once completed and tested, this new life center (the ENS) becomes responsible for the development of the central nervous system (CNS). The CNS must ultimately learn to assume responsibility for mobility and protection of the ENS in its many external environments. The ENS receives its intelligence from its parent's genes; the CNS receives its intelligence from its own experience in the outside world.

These processes of the ENS are to manage the digestion system, manage the generation of energy, manage the heart pump and circulation of nutrients in the blood, and manage the growth activities of the central nervous system (CNS). The awareness of the management of all life process indicates that the ENS has the responsibility to apply limitations to the activities of the CNS. This set of limitations makes sense when the background of the Human animal with its genetic history is allowed to learn to adapt to new environmental challenges, as long as its new interests take into account life support of the ENS.

When changes represent the interest of the CNS beyond the limits of the present need of the Human being, then the ENS reduces energy to the activity of the CNS. With prolonged loss of energy, the organism will likely express itself with some form of discomfort. An example of this is the lack of energy and attentiveness to one's occupation when it no longer interests the individual. This functionality of the ENS, it seems to us, is demonstrating the use of a learning process of "trial and learn" using one's own energy. This gives us a clue for use of the same learning process when acquiring any form of intelligence.

Our Single Center of Intelligence

It may surprise some people that there is a combination of two systems with natural intelligence in the Human body—ENS with its animal brain sitting at the top of the spinal column, and the CNS with its sensory brain, empty at birth but growing over time into the same skull cavity. This combination of two separate brains with the functionality of a single center of intelligence stores and fills the cavity with its neurological experience from inside and also from the outside world.

Remember, that the ENS has had millions of years to learn and store its experience, to meet new challenges, and bring it up to date. So, the ENS with its experience becomes the coach, knowing what it needs to achieve, and how it wants to accomplish its objective. Only the details of the learning process are left to the organism to make, and they are monitored by the ENS to evaluate the amount of energy given in support of this process. So we have arrived at a point where we have an idea of what there is in the way of an over all human intelligence system, but now let's explore how it works.

Human ideas of progress come from nature, even though we like to think we are inventors. One of those ideas is the use of systems. We know that there are various types of systems, one of which is a Closed System (CS). A CS is one in which the system is self sustaining—once started, it perpetuates itself until there is no more life to support. In Human Nature we have a closed system. The sun is our source of energy, plant life converts the sun's energy to food, the food is digested by the gut and converted to chemical energy with the liquid nutrients pumped throughout the body. Next the waste products are eliminated from plants and animals as fertilizer, and the cycle automatically begins again with the sun's energy.

There is much more to understand how the two systems— ENS and CNS—communicate with each other, and operate in sync, as a single center of intelligence. However, communications operate at millisecond speed in order to coordinate information from one system to another system. Suffice it to say that normally there is a communication system in each of us that makes constant inter-system communication possible at millisecond speed. At this high speed of coordinate communications, the movements of external and internal muscles appear to move as a single unit when either one is stimulated.

There is one exception that may be of interest to some. The CNS tires from all the physical activity. The sensory information it receives to sort out and store for memory goes to sleep each day and rests. On the other hand, after the CNS goes to sleep, the ENS continues to send messages of feeling to the sleeping CNS, and it is then that we have our metaphoric dream, which we are often unable to understand.

We know now that the gut has over 80% of all serotonin in the body and that gut-to-head communication can have a calming affect upon us and help reduce stress. Baba Shiv, professor of marketing and director of the Strategic Marketing Management Executive Program at the Stanford Graduate School of Business, suggests that our best decisions are made in the morning when our natural levels of serotonin are the highest, following high gut-to-head communication during deep sleep at night.

There are many theories about metaphoric dreams, and we will share ours. Dreams are rarely focused on the outside world, but rather are about our inner state. If family or close friends are used as characters in a dream and if they are positive, the message generally indicates a feeling of fullness in your life. And if the dream character symbols are negative, the message generally indicates feelings of emptiness in your life, stress, worry—unfinished 'business'. In this way, we see that the ENS feeds messages to the sleeping CNS and influences the meaning of our dreams. This is not to say that the ENS never has a resting phase, for it does, but it continues to be active and communicates during part of the CNS dream cycle.

> "Nights through dreams tell the myths forgotten by the day."
>
> — C.G. Jung in *Memories, Dreams, Reflections*

Trial and Learn

There is very little chance, maybe none, that a strong Intuitional Intelligence can be built without some past experience with the animal brain—its ENS—combined with the sensory brain and its CNS. This combination of logic and nature's evaluation (gut feelings) provides the status of intelligence for the best judgment an individual will be able to make. The goal of the *Trial and Learn* process must be initiated as soon as possible after birth in order to give a child the best intuition to solve the personal and the cultural problems he/she will face.

But there are some major blocks in our cultural life today that sets limits on the development of the *trial and learn* process. Most cultures would have to start from scratch to achieve an environment conducive to body-mind unity and support of Human Nature. 'From scratch' would mean examining all possible pressures against Human Nature's individual needs for freedom and acceptance, and getting rid of all the pressures from every source that work against these two principles. Ideally the list of these pressures to eliminate involves the underpinnings of most societies where disparate laws of Human mind and body are related to some religious faith, and wherein civil laws rest on religious law, whether or not there is any verbal reference to its presence. This situation is the major problem, which if solved, would help solve problems related to learning and education, tax laws, medical expense, incarceration, governance, etc.

The details of the task to free Human Nature (and thus the *trial and learn* process inherit in our instincts) make it appear impossible at a glance: To reject religious law, to rewrite civil law, and to accept natural law, in order to free the instinctual content of natural law. Such an enormous change would be unthinkable to many as one would seem to need to accept the fact that there had never been an arching external power or presence that loved and cared for Human life on this earth. With this rejection of religious law, one might say that if there was an external power elsewhere that was looking over us, there was never any evidence to show its presence—thus it has always been attached to 'faith'.

"Encouraging people to simply believe without any personal validation or direct-experience is antithetical to consciousness of the Truth. Such "faith-based" thinking undermines reason, responsibility, a respect for fact, open-mindedness, and even common sense."

—Peter Ralston in Pursuing Consciousness

So here we have two points of view, one is to put all our trust in a *faith-based* religious doctrines and the second is to reject and discard religion in favor of following one's instincts as self regulatory and as a valuable inner guide. But wait, are we limited to only these two options? There is another point of view concerning religion and religious law that would support the importance of human instincts and yet not necessitate the giving up of the idea of an external power—some Divine intelligence. This third way of viewing would be that an external Divine power is also built within us (man being made in the image of God). That is to say, our internal gut feeling intelligence connected to our Human Nature is a part of the Divine external power and may therefore be trusted to guide us experientially. With this view, we understand that it is our inner nature and instinctual gut feeling center (the direct feeling experience of the second brain) rather than our thinking brain (keeping score of the religious "faith-based" doctrines) that is our strongest connection to the Divine energy. And then we may be able to free our Human Nature and at the same time, if desired, continue to embrace the understanding of an external Divine energy—just one that is never absolutely understood by the thinking brain as we have been led to believe by non-gnostic religions.

21

We take up this issue of viewing religious and spiritual ideas from an internal point of view in a later essay in Part 4 of this book. We give you an example of how this change from the external God (related to the thinking brain without instinctual awareness) to the internal Human Nature (related to our gut instinctual intelligence with the thinking brain in unity with it) changes religious thinking to be more honest and directly experiential, thus actually useful to Human life and wellness. The example that we will discuss is on the subject of redemption and you will see that if you include the instincts to interpret redemption, it is quite useful in a psychological way to problem solving in day-to-day Human life. Some modern religious groups, such as the Unitarians, are beginning to include the importance of instinctual awareness in their spiritual teachings and believe that significant meaning and value can be discovered in life on earth. Of course, some Eastern spiritual systems have long been including Human gut instincts in their teachings, for instance some forms of Yoga revere the use of the belly (Hara as Breath of Life) as the center of life and spiritual knowledge. But we propose that much is needed to make this shift to inner Divine awareness clear in the more fundamental religious groups that are prevalent in today's cultures, and to unite the gut and head brain intelligence.

We view science and religion as one. When you look at the heart of what science discovers about our Human existence and when you view religion and spiritual beliefs from an inner point of view, you see that they are one and the same in what they are telling us about ourselves. When science had developed the tools to look and physically examine the inside of the Human anatomy, it found two separate brains with two neurological systems providing energy of life to a body, mind, and a spirit of life. It suddenly became clear that there was no place for fundamentalist religions that do not embrace the science of the Human Beings, who are equipped by nature at birth to take care of themselves and each other. Without this functional system or way of viewing ourselves to organize our lives that is in harmony with our Human Nature, the species could ultimately destroy itself.

Growing and Learning

We have been impressed by the way a good coach handles a football team. When a student wants to play on the team but has no previous experience in the game, the coach will watch him in practice show his stuff: how he uses his body, how he thinks, and how he manages his energy. When the coach is satisfied with the student's determination and potential to play football, he will discuss a position appropriate to satisfy the student's expectations, and help him grow over time in that position. If the student learns over time that he is losing interest in his choice of activity, and quits the game, he has learned an important lesson that playing football was not what he thought it was and was not satisfying his needs.

The essential point we're trying to make here is that growing and learning rarely follow in a strait line, and are never mistakes. In *The Rise: Creativity, the Gift of Failure, and the Search for Mastery* published in 2015, Sarah Lewis, an assistant professor of the History of Art and Architecture and of African and African American Studies at Harvard University, explores how teaching our children the importance of learning to push forward despite failure has throughout history been of tremendous importance in learning to be successful in life, in

23

achieving mastery in an area or subject, and in having what she calls grit or being "gutsy".

What better way could we teach our children the importance of learning to push forward despite failure than to openly embrace in the education system *Trial and Learn* as our truly only human learning process. In doing so, we would eliminate the stigma of failure and view it as an important part of the process of learning.

We learn much more from *Trial and Learn* than from guessing, and expecting always to be correct with our choices. The satisfying aspect of being 'wrong' in this incident will be stored in your memory, and can surface often with a chuckle—again and again—to steer your mind away from repeating it in the future. The idea is that when you choose experience, you are committing your own time, energy, and interest, and not what someone else has instructed you to do. If what you have learned from your experience was what you wanted to know or do, you have taken a step toward building confidence in your self with more energy to try again. If you didn't learn what you wanted to know or do, you have learned to be more cautious with your curiosity— more careful with your intuition.

The Principles of Learning

We now have an idea of how the Human intelligence system works, however we need to expand upon it, and add some tools that we have not mentioned. So, what do we have to work with?

We have two areas of intelligence:

1. The sensory brain is for storage of its experiential history of its outside world, and its central nervous system (CNS) that is attached to electrochemical sensors throughout the external body. The CNS is placed in areas of the body where it functionally cooperates with the animal brain. The animal brain manages all electrochemical functions within the gut, and its enteric nervous system (ENS).

2. The ENS is designed to digest the food, to furnish and circulate energy throughout the entire organism, and has the function of recording and storing the functional history of the quality of life of the entire organism as a reference—the impact on it of its current and past experience.

We need to interject here something important. We are saying that we must have both the CNS and ENS to fully function and to develop intuitive intelligence. The CNS must develop both the physical and intellectual skills necessary for living and the ENS provides the instinctual need awareness of life. Without the CNS, the ENS would function without any outer awareness and direction; and without the ENS, the CNS may function contrary to the needs of the person and the affects upon the inner needs of the person. An example of this is in the task of the baby learning to walk. Both the mental and physical aspects of the CNS must be developed for the baby to experiment and learn this process, and also the baby uses his/her instinctual awareness of the ENS in the process. The CNS expresses its views of the details of experience in its environmental language of thinking—environmental standards and physical abilities. ENS expresses its views of the same details but with the feelings of the environmental impact on the quality of life that it is experiencing.

This duality of intelligence furnishes us two valuable centers of reference, which can help us to individually and collectively control our own inner needs without any mystical power from the outside world. The inner needs of quality of life for the Human animal is not switched on/off but much like the gas gauge in your automobile, allows for variations of *empty* or *full feelings* of life to be adjusted by the individual.

Where fear, stress, and disaster occur in the life of a Human is when the animal is denied the duality of necessity, *acceptance* and *control* (attention and freedom). This is sadly when animals are willing to end life. With no hope of freedom, alone with no attention from a desired other, and no hope of change they experience an empty life. We have discussed in our first book the likely possibility that an empty life, if not corrected, will first develop signs of illness in the gut or elsewhere in the body; and if not treated, will grow to destroy the organism. "The prospect of an empty life, like an empty gas-tank, will take us nowhere without attention."

Early childhood demonstrates the struggle of the Human Being in achieving the necessities of its environment. It is using its own early energy to try to copy what it touches, sees, and hears, and that energy is generated by its own instincts, its ENS. Later on it will be able to see and hear beyond the confines of its birth environment when it will seek more control and acceptance from strangers. It is this experience of *trial and learn* that can form a balance between self-control and self-acceptance, a positive self-image, and a full life registers on its 'gas gauge' or gut feelings of emptiness and fullness.

26

Promoting Gut Feeling Awareness in the Classroom

We may all agree that science now has the tools to understand the intelligence with which we have to individually begin life at birth. The important task ahead is to make the most of our beginnings in an environment such as an educational institution when it is not always of the child's own choice to be there. Children often first attend school to please their parents and if this decision is never one that fulfills their own needs, it can partially separate him/her from the necessary instinctual intelligence with which he/her was born. The school environment all to often fosters less feeling intelligence to balance thinking intelligence. This condition weakens the balance between the two functional systems, produces less energy, produces empty feelings in the gut and a distorted ability to make good judgments, experiences difficulty in relationships with others, and experiences some type of illness if the imbalance continues.

It may surprise you that we advocate beginning the learning process about multiple brains in very early childhood. From our work as educators of both the gut and head brains (a two brain system), we would like to make these very brief suggestions for activities and time frames for education and promotion of self-awareness skills of the intelligence of our multiple brains:

Pre-school—Time to build a positive self-image and body awareness: watch and listen to the child, and begin an early simple dialog about inner gut feelings (emptiness and fullness) and needs of Control and Acceptance (C/A), use language appropriate for age of child. (Begin art, dance, music, body movement in small groups).

<u>Entering School</u>—Reinforce C/A: Promote projects of individual interests and keep track of individual's energy levels in relation to specific activities. Provide special attention to troubled students—apply use of Somatic Reflection Process to troubled students when necessary. (Continue the arts.)

<u>Ages (6-10)</u>— Continue dialog about inner feelings and inner needs. Explore together the difference in thinking and feeling in the body, in small groups. We suggest that a group discussion is held each morning as a "check in" for each student on their gut feelings. This is very important in coaching the child to direct his/her own learning. Continue to reinforce C/A: Introduce leveled academic skills of reading, writing, mathematics, and spelling around relevant topics and subjects to students (using a student-centered learning approach). Begin creative projects related to individual interests, such as music (voice or instrumental), dance, sports (individual or team), painting, sketching (art), animal care, construction, other subjects of students' interests, etc.

<u>Ages (10-16)</u>—Group Discussion: Self image, reflections on feelings and memories, sexuality, etc. This is an important age for presentation of individual work with others in groups (remember that one of our important Human instinctual needs is to feel acceptance and be social). Career exploration begins from the reference of inner needs fulfillment, along with continued academic skill development and exploration of the arts. Use of Somatic Reflection Process for career exploration and self-awareness.

In addition to reading, writing, and arithmetic, all kids need to learn self-awareness, self-regulation, and communication as part of their core curriculum. Just as we teach history and geography, we need to teach children how their brains and bodies work. For adults and children alike, being in control of ourselves requires becoming familiar with our inner world and accurately identifying what scares, upsets, or delights us."

— Bessel A. van der Kolk in *The Body Keeps the Score: Brain, Mind, and Body in the Healing of Trauma*

Instinctual Awareness Helps Children Learn

We are proposing the use of the Somatic Reflection Process (or some part of its use) in the classrooms at early ages for children (both with small groups and with individuals). It is our experience that the use of this technique can vastly assist people in accessing their gut instincts to become aware of their two inner instinctual needs of acceptance and control. This has been noted in our clinical studies to begin the process of learning to follow ones inner guide—the feelings in our guts—to increase self-awareness, intuition, and body-mind unity for wellness. And we have found this technique to work cross-culturally.

We have found that with person's of all ages, without becoming aware of their gut feelings and doing some serious reflection to uncover the impact of life upon them, there are certain learning processes that easily become stagnant. For instance, it takes some instinctual awareness to let go of outdated ways of thinking (particularly about what one can and can not do) that do not serve the person's needs and cause one to be inflexible, even inactive, and unable to allow oneself to have new experiences. There is as aspect of a need for flexibility in the *trial and learn* process that is vital to learning from new experience. Another example of important learning that is only possible with the use of instinctual awareness reflection is in learning more about ones inner psyche, emotional intelligence skills, and in developing an Intuitional Intelligence. Becoming aware of our instincts is the key to self-awareness and intuitive thought based on the input of the knowledge of the impact of our experiences upon us and allows us to develop as individuals in creative ways.

We have made a list of learning skills and personality traits possible to enhance through exploring the awareness of the two instinctual needs of acceptance (attention) and control of one's one responses (freedom). This is followed by a list of skills and traits enhanced through the combination of the awareness of both of these instinctual needs.

ACCEPTANCE:

- Self-Awareness (respect for Self)
- High ability for Self care
- Openness to Others (respect for and trust of others)
- Social fulfillment (feeling connected to others)
- Compassion for self and other
- Ability to work well with others of all ages

CONTROL:

- Open Mindedness (willing to have new experiences)

- Flexibility (ability to learn from *trial and learn*)
- Conscientiousness (for self-discipline and self-care)

FROM BOTH ACCEPTANCE AND CONTROL:

- Higher Intuitional Intelligence
- Individuality and Self-Expression
- A Sense of Universal Connectedness
- Awareness of Mind/Body Connection
- Higher Skills in Communication of Feelings
- Recognition of One's Own Needs and Feelings and of Other People's Needs and Feelings
- Enhances Self-Care Abilities
- Recognition of Self Motivations (knows and continues to explore what is one's passion)
- Compassion for Self and Others

On Educating Our Inner Garden

When we plant a garden, we carefully place our seeds in a well-nurtured environment. We give the seeds the essentials to help them grow into what they are designed to be. We do not take on the task of making the seeds become a tomato or sunflower, for we trust that they each know exactly what they are to become. We trust that under the right conditions, they will become the best they can be of exactly what it is they are designed to be. But with the Human Being, we may start out with this same understanding—feeding, and loving, and allowing the infant to develop on its own. However, we soon decide that we know more of what the child should become than the child knows itself. Yes, we know it will develop into the body of a person and the qualities of a Human Being, but what of the moral character, knowledge and self-awareness of the Human Being. We are quick to take up the responsibility to manage the child's outer ego personality, "for it's own good".

At what age do we normally take over and manage the growth of the child into our ideal person rather than continuing to observe and nurture it's own innate self-awareness and self-regulated direction? A year old? 6 months? Earlier still? Surely we take over long before we send the child to school to learn the lessons we think should be learned to develop and live in this world.

But of course, we understand that children need to learn how to function in the man-made world, just as wild mammals of other species are often taught to learn to function in their natural world by their parents. It is the parent's job to do so. But, we as Human Beings often forget that there is an inner direction of the Human Being, a daemon as James Hillman spoke of in *The Soul's Code*, that has far greater chance to successfully develop and function than anything we could think up and superimpose upon the person.

How many of us wonder what we would be as adults if we had been naturally supported to grow from an awareness within ourselves rather than from the awareness outside of ourselves. That is to say, what would we be if parents and the culture fertilized their little seeds—us—organically rather than artificially, and cared about our inner feelings rather than our behavior. The good news is, there is no time like the present, at any age, to fertilize your own garden of the Self and engage your instincts to guide you through *Trail and Learn* and increase your Intuitional Intelligence.

Learning to Read the Feeling Gauge In Your Gut!

We offer the following discussion and diagrams on feeling into your gut as a gauge of your instinctual needs—acceptance and control of one's own responses (freedom). We have placed this here in the second chapter so readers may better understand this core experience of the instincts, as it underlies all our further discussions on the gut brain and on developing Intuitional Intelligence that we present in this book. The three diagrams are intended as educational materials that may be used in the classroom, in counseling sessions, and by the general reader. Often, we find that pictures help us in understanding complicated psychological theory and make it possible to apply them to improving our daily lives.

Much has been written on emotional eating and dieting. We think we all now can agree that there is a direct correlation between eating to fill emotional emptiness and overeating to fill what we think is hunger. It is very difficult to separate the feeling of emptiness in our guts caused by hunger from the emptiness that causes emotional eating. But we need to learn how (and certainly can learn) to do this if we are going to be healthy and truly happy people. When we feel emptiness in our guts, empty and alone, then we often grab comfort food to fill this emptiness. Because it is not what will really fill this type of emptiness (emotional), we are not truly satisfied stuffing ourselves with food (even though it is enjoyable at the time) and we keep eating to attempt to fill it, often resulting in unwanted weight gain. This brings three questions to mind:

1. What will fill this emotional emptiness in the pit of our stomachs?
2. What are the instinctual needs that are often confused for the need of food in gut feelings of emptiness and fullness?
3. What is the gut trying to tell us about our needs?

These are such simple and important questions that we might wonder why more people are not addressing them. Doesn't this affect us all? Of course it does and the answers may surprise you.

As we have explained in the first essay, the gut is a brain, a center of intelligence. It has much more to tell us about ourselves than when we need food and when we do not. It isn't a far step from the awareness of emotional eating to the understanding that our gut feeling of emptiness (feeling empty and alone) is not really a gauge of the need to eat food but a gauge of the need for more basic psychological needs. We find it important for people to center their awareness on filling the emotional needs reflected in the gut feelings of emptiness and fullness while working on improving their diets. Both emotional needs and diet are equally important and work together to improve health and wellness.

Are Gut Feelings Really in the Gut?

People often write us and ask us if gut feelings are really in the gut. The source of gut feelings are a bit confusing to many

34

people. Once we become aware of our gut feelings and begin to exercise our use of this powerful intelligence, our energy releases from the Hara upward and is in communication with the rest of our body and thinking brain. The feeling from our gut then releases energy in other parts of our body like the heart. Because this communication from the gut is so fast, at this point, it can be difficult to tell where the energy and information, the intuition that arises, first began.

We can, of course, become more aware of our gut feelings and trace our insights and Intuitional Intelligence to the original gut response in the Hara or belly area. As a person begins to focus on gut feelings of emptiness and fullness (once again, not to be mistaken with a need for food intake), it becomes clearer and clearer that the gut feelings are our own response to the impact of life upon us and are connected to all of Nature.

Understanding Your Gut Feelings and What They Are Telling You

To assist you in understanding this feeling gauge in the gut, we have drawn the three diagrams on the following pages and hope you find them useful in exploring your gut feelings and the instinctual needs connected to these gut responses. These diagrams are an attempt to help give a picture of this process of reflection on gut feelings and what your feelings are telling you about your needs and life energy. It is, however, rather an over simplification of our gut feeling experience. Feel free to use these as educational materials in the classroom or with individuals.

Understanding Your Gut Feelings and What They Are Telling You About _____

(You fill in the blank, ie "a love relationship", "your job", "a career decision", "a business investment", etc.)

Feel Into The Gauge in Your Gut
Imagine you have something like a gas gauge in your gut that registers how empty or full you feel from moment-to-moment concerning two instinctual needs of Acceptance From Others and of Control of One's Own Reponses to Life (your free, authentic response). Where are you today?

EMPTY   FULL

Combine that with the teeter-totter in your gut:
1. Feeling Full, absolute 100% (or near). When our two basic needs of feeling accepted and in control of our own responses to life are in balance, then we feel full in our gut feelings (loved for who we are; and our life, career, or business decisions appear to have the opportunity for us to feel accepted through our own will), and we are full of energy and often feel a connection to a divine "Presence" and Intuitive Intelligence.

ACCEPTANCE————————————CONTROL (freedom)

The diagram above shows the gauge in our gut as it registers when our needs for acceptance and control are in balance (our gut feelings of emptiness and fullness).

----

2. Feeling Half Full (but not 100% full), often also aware of a feeling of underlying emptiness for lack of our need for control of our own responses) Here our basic need for control of our own responses is out of balance, although we have some degree of the feeling of acceptance and attention from others. We may be playing a role of who we think we need to be for acceptance from others (perhaps for the benefit of a particular important person to us or from old outdated tapes in our head of who we think we need to be in order to not be alone and to be acceptable.) The emptiness is that we are not feeling our own sense of freedom to be ourselves so we do not feel loved for who we truly are. In that case, we may never show others who we truly are until a crisis or breakup and we may be rejected in the long run because the most natural part of ourselves is hidden and never offered. If we reflect back, we often see it was our role that was rejected in relationships, not our true selves. If you feel this emptiness, you need to take some control and at least voice your needs to someone you trust, even if it is a journal. Being aware of your gut feelings is an important beginning to balance.

ACCEPTANCE

CONTROL (freedom)

This diagram demonstrates when a person is out of balance in that the need for acceptance (attention and social) is met but a sense of control (freedom to respond naturally as one feels) is not met.

---

3. Feeling Half Full (but not 100% full), often also aware of some feeling of underlying emptiness for lack of our need for acceptance from others)
Here our basic need for acceptance from connection to others is out of balance, although we have some degree of the full feeling of being in control of our own responses to life. We may feel we have taken some necessary control to respond from our own needs and perspective but have lost acceptance from others. We may feel some aloneness and often this feels okay, at least for a while. Othertimes, we feel we have gone out too far on a limb and need to take other's needs into account so we gain the acceptance and connection to others that we need. This is where we may feel some risk in business, but also a feeling of necessity to go forward with our gut feelings and intutitive ideas resulting from our gut and head conversing. Love relationships may be strained at times with this gauging, unless both of you or the group you have joined agrees to accept the free will of each other as individuals and you work on communication together. Here again, expressing to an accepting indiviual your needs and feeling of aloneness in taking the control in your life that you have felt necessary is very important in coming to a place of balance, reducing stress, and healthy decision-making.
Remember, you have taken freedom in your life, what you need now is acceptance and your gut is telling you.

CONTROL (freedom)

ACCEPTANCE

This diagram demonstrates when a person is out of balance in that a sense of control (freedom to respond naturally as one feels) is met but the need for a sense of acceptance (attention and social) is not met.

There are, of course, other scenarios beyond the three we have diagrammed, but these are the three we have seen most often in counseling. The forth that is unfortunately experienced by most of us at one dark and difficult time or another in our lives, but not included here, is a feeling of nearly 100% both the lack of acceptance and lack of control in our lives. We suppose in that case, the teeter-totter would be pictured upside down.

We suggest that you take a few quiet minutes, if you have not already done so, to review these diagrams carefully and to reflect somatically within your own gut feelings to determine the impact of life upon you at this moment. What is the gauge in your gut registering? If you feel a little (or a lot) empty, is it an issue of acceptance and attention needs or is it control and freedom needs or is it both? Understanding this material on a gut feeling response level will greatly enhance your ability to understand the complex theories presented in this book.

How To Become Aware of Gut Feelings To Overcome Stress

Understanding the 12 keys presented in this chapter will help you successfully navigate through your awareness of your own gut intelligence. With these keys, you may begin to use your gut feelings as an inner guide to accompany your thinking brain decisions. In this chapter, we talk about how the awareness of your gut feelings will help you in relieving stress in your inner life so that you may be clear to further develop your Intuitional Intelligence. While there are people who work well under some pressure, remember that being over stressed blocks our Intuitional Intelligence.

These 12 keys reflect the responses of hundreds of people that we worked with in a clinical counseling setting and also later in a research study at Sonoma State University in 2005. They have been greatly expanded from a narrative in our first book *What's Behind Your Belly Button?* They are included here as a useful summary and as an example of educational material to understand the new psychology of gut intelligence.

The Psychology of Gut Intelligence is a new field of study and research. Many people are still baffled as to how to even begin to understand our second brain in our bellies. Our 2005 research study in depth psychology found that listening to the voice of your gut can lead people to have a more beneficial life experience with stress reduction and more decisive choices that benefit both the culture and the individual person. We hope that these keys presented below will help you in understanding your gut instincts for dealing with emotional stress and increasing wellness. If you follow these keys, you will be on your way to unifying your two brains to work together to help you make healthy life-decisions and to reduce stress in your life.

We need to be ready to dispense with what is no longer useful and gather new skills to evolve into our future being. When our head and gut brains are united, then our Intuitional Intelligence

40

will flourish and counsel us to avoid hoarding on all levels. Physical plane hoarding is dangerous, but emotional and mental hoarding can get one into real trouble and take away our life energy and ability to make healthy decisions. The following 12 keys are the principles behind The Somatic Reflection Process, a technique to assist you in clearing out your emotional and mental storage units. Understanding the following 12 keys will help you begin to disperse what has crystallized and flow past all obstructions.

12 Keys to Understand Your Gut Instincts and Overcome Emotional Stress

1. The Hara or gut is the instinctual response center and we feel in our gut either empty or full or somewhere in the middle. Imagine a gauge in your gut at all times (see diagrams on pages 35-39).

2. We feel a full feeling in our gut region of the body when our instinctual needs are met and an empty feeling when they are not met. We are not talking about the feeling of full-empty from food intake, but from more psychological instinctual needs (although these are somewhat similar in feeling). We often do get our feelings of hunger and our more emotional instinctual needs confused and therefore may over-eat to try to fill the emptiness we feel psychologically. These instincts are psychological not in the sense of the use of our logical mind but in our needs as human beings.

3. We have two instinctual needs that the gut registers—the need to feel accepted (attention) and the need to be in control of our own responses to life (freedom). These two needs must

41

be constantly in balance and too much of one without the other leaves us empty.

Ask yourself: How do I feel in my gut right now? Is my gut gauge on empty or full or in between feeling only a little empty, half full or half empty? If you feel a little empty in your gut, then feel into this emptiness and we will explore to see if it relates to your need for acceptance or for control. This is a good place to begin the Somatic Reflection Process to explore what the emptiness is about.

4. When we have both of these instinctive needs met, we feel full and thus energized; and when we have neither met, we feel empty and often experience some symptoms of stress in the body, which may even lead to dis-ease.

5. The gut response does not depend on the thinking brain as the gut is an independent brain of its own. It can, of course, be greatly affected by the thinking brain, and vice-versa. (Gut flora research has validated the affects that the head and gut have upon each other in biological health studies.)

6. We work both consciously and unconsciously to keep these two instinctual needs in balance at all times.

7. We need to have a balanced and conscious dialog between our gut responses and head responses so we can use our thinking brain to make the appropriate decisions and responses in the external world and to try to fill these two important instinctual needs in appropriate and successful ways.

8. When we are unconscious of our gut responses, our thinking brain will often use a system of thought it has picked up (perhaps from an authority like a parent, teacher or even a religious interpretation) and applies it as a judgment about the feeling in our gut. This is what happens when we have an emotion like guilt or depression. We feel empty because our

42

needs are not met and our thinking brain attaches a thought to the emptiness and a lack of our fulfillment like "It is all my fault for being too stupid or too small or too incompetent, etc." or "I am not capable of doing anything to make this work or be better" or "I am not worthy or deserving", thus we have guilt or fear and or other difficult emotions.

Ask yourself: Does the emptiness that I am feeling have anything to do with a judgment I am carrying about myself? To answer this question, it is helpful to see if an image of a face comes to your awareness as you center your awareness on your empty feeling. If not, then it may help to imagine the faces of those close to you and check your gut feelings to see if you have any feeling of emptiness related to anyone you presently know. If not, you may try going back in time in your awareness to find where or who the emptiness relates to. If you find the person it relates to in the present, remember that this person may or may not hold the judgment you have taken as you may be triggered back into your past experiences and this will require more somatic reflection. If you are taking on a judgment from someone else about you, then you are most likely now experiencing a combination of logic (the judgment) and feeling of emptiness. This becomes an emotion like guilt or shame and may become even an emotion like fear of the future or anger in defense of who you now think you could be.

9. The emotional feelings are not pure feelings of emptiness or fullness anymore, as they now have the thinking component mixed in them. And these thinking-feelings or emotions are mostly felt in other parts of our bodies above our Hara, between our head brain and gut brain. If you examine your emotional feelings, you can always find a thinking element to them. And if you trace the somatic feeling aspect only, it goes

43

directly and purely to the gut as a feeling of emptiness or fullness. The gut is the source of all feeling and feeling memory. _Ask yourself_: Do I feel some emotions underlying my emptiness?

10. Generally, the only way we can unravel an inaccurate thinking judgment and the resulting emotional stress, is to reflect back to the source of when the thinking head first applied this very same judgment and find the actual source or as close to it as possible. And the key to finding this first experience is through somatic reflection on the gut feeling of emptiness and fullness (using the Somatic Reflection Process complete protocol) not through just trying to think back on the details of our lives.

Ask yourself? Have I ever felt this way before? It is important to center on the gut feeling of emptiness (or fullness if it is a positive trigger feeling you want to remember fully) and ask yourself if you have ever felt this way before. Keep working back in time as you center on this feeling until you get very early in life. It will surprise you how this feeling has been with you a long time, shape shifting the details but always keeping the same core judgment and emotion all the way into the present time. You will see that the present situation is often simply a trigger of an early experience and it is necessary to become conscious of this initial feeling experience to disperse the emptiness and stress.

11. Once we find this original experience in which we started the "tape" that plays over and over in our heads saying that we are at fault, powerless, too needy, unlovable, etc., then we can lift the sentence we have placed on ourselves and on our feelings. We can then begin to see ourselves clearer and make healthy decisions, feeling more in control of our own responses

to life. We begin to use our thinking head to follow our instinctual needs and fulfill our true Human Nature.

12. Reflection on the gut voice helps us to be more mindful of our caring nature and thus be more caring of others. And with the new awareness of our gut responses and needs that we acquire through reflection on our instinctual gut responses, we are able to live a more caring and healthy life, with the thinking head finally conscious and listening more clearly to the responses that are our path to our most reliable and authentic self—our gut instinctual feelings in our body.

The Mysteries of Human Instincts and Behavior

We have looked in our first chapter at how Human instincts are self-regulatory and how they provide an important *Trial and Learn* process to guide us and help us evolve. Why aren't we encouraging the use of the instincts beyond birth—especially in the learning process in the early years of life, when learning is at its peak? And what has the affect been upon our Humanity that we have been so neglectful of our instinctual awareness?
In this chapter, we further explore how the gut instincts and thinking brain must have experience working together for Human life to exist and to evolve. We propose that the human species will do so despite the marginalization of the gut brain by cultures throughout modern history.

No one can deny the obvious fact that Human Nature continually demonstrates behavior throughout history that is more like that of lesser members of the animal species rather than one of superior intelligence and understanding. We seem to have on the one hand the capacity to love and care for each other—Humans and other members of the animal kingdom—and yet on the other hand quickly reverse our behavior to that of anger, hatred, war and destruction. Because of these qualities of behavior and the mysteries with accompanied guesses from professionals about the causes of these personality perturbations, mankind has been convinced over eons of time that we are the possessors of inerasable aspects of our animal instincts of both good and evil. Most people are therefore under the impression that we need external powers of influence, like religion and imposed moral codes, to regulate our behavior in order to produce more good than evil.

It is this very idea that Humans need regulation from external sources that we see as having gotten us into trouble as Human beings—not our Human Nature itself. We think the history of this misconception is important to trace, so that we understand how we got here and what needs to be done to change this misconception and further educate our Humanity. So let us explore this misconception about our Human Nature.

Why Are We Not Educating Our Instincts?

It became clear to us that prior to our counseling clinical work with gut feelings, the conscious use of this gut intelligence was never before cultivated in Human society. By this we mean that there has never been a culture in history based on uniting both the thinking and gut brain intelligence. We began this book by discussing the importance of instincts in the learning process and many other aspects of Human growth and development starting with conception. Yet, as we get into the subject of instincts, we find that we face the question; "Why aren't we encouraging the use of the instincts beyond birth—especially in the learning process in the early years of life, when learning is at its peak?"

Our answer suggests that at some time quite recently in Human history (and to this day), it has been decided that in order to find dependable 'good' behavior in Human Nature, it is necessary to control Human Natures' "evil" behavior by inventing external forces to keep it in check. So we find that we are surrounded by arbitrary civil laws and religious laws, which insist that natural law be distorted to conform to a set of ethical and moral standards. Kind of dumb is it not? How does anyone change natural laws? Does anyone who can think clearly as we look at the results of this concoction believe that this scheme is working? Fortunately, modern science has now come to the rescue furnishing convincing evidence that Human Nature has the intelligence to control its self.

To begin to deal with Human learning as a process of animal need for the Human individual is to change our cultural focus of attention from the plethora of external Human achievements to the inner world of Human necessity. We think this change involves our Human feelings and it will lead us in finding through some serious self-reflection elements of emptiness that we have ignored—overwhelmed by the externally focused senses. Many people today feel that something is wrong with our inner satisfaction with life but few have any notion of what to do about it or where to look for a solution.

To include the ancient animal intelligence—a powerful natural inner intelligence with which the Human animal is born—with the essential instincts is presently sure to be a disturbing subject for many people who have marginalized the importance of their instincts. Such a change is necessary, however, to free those "devilish" instincts, which have now been discovered by both clinical and neurological research to be essential to accurate Human learning needs, and which we as a species are presently denying. The results of these efforts of both experience and research now demand a new and more accurate functional image (way of viewing) of our *homo sapient* nature.

In order to produce a more healthy and accurate understanding of the animal mind and body intelligence, thinking and feeling together—the intuition—requires experience with these basic tools for healthy and accurate problem solving (learning) for the newborn, older children, and adults as they mature.

From the amalgam of modern science now available, intuition, and personal experience, we conclude that most cultures have never consciously integrated the two brains with their nervous systems. Therefore, we as educators are not effectively using this Second Brain—the animal brain. "We are not effectively applying and consciously using the brains we were born with!" And many cultures are still denying the obvious fact that Humans are members of the animal kingdom.

Until the latter part of the 20th Century, there was little interest from our modern world (so focused on logic and the head brain) in the digestive system as a center of functional intelligence—intelligence that could play a dominate role in the learning process and the well-being of Humans as members of

48

the animal kingdom. The notion of the importance of the gut as a center of intelligence was left years ago prior to our modern cultures. Any attempt to revive the gut's place of importance has been rejected until recently. What is suspected is that the gut—the ancient animal brain with its enteric nervous system (ENS)—and perhaps the whole body has somehow been mistakenly viewed as the disruptive force that interferes with the management of Human behavior.

The Discovery Process

As we have previously pointed out, Dr. Michael Gershon's published work with the Enteric Nervous System, *The Second Brain*, (1998), alerted us to the profound importance of a gut brain to all life processes including learning and Human behavior. Once we could form a new image of the Human system based on the new neurological science he discovered, we then could re-examine Human behavior relative to this new functional model. We were also significantly aided in our initial structure of the early model by the research of Lise Eliot, Ph. D, which led us through the process of *How The Brain and Mind Develop in the First Five Years of Life*. (1999).

A new education plan (to take the place of the version of the old British plan that we still use in the West) that we propose is a *Learning* plan and it is designed to provide a well-balanced mind using all the intuitive intelligence the mind can produce, which satisfies its needs and that of the culture. Such a mind must include the use of the animal brain—the intelligence of the brain it was born with—including the instincts. Individual minds must live in environments of Freedom and Attention in

49

order to have the opportunity to learn to control its Self through experience with others—from birth until death.

With both neurological research and experience combined together to form a new functional (useable) image of Human Nature (a model of how Human Nature works), we found that much of the instinctive disruption that has been observed of Human behavior in the past, has been the result of external pressures imposed on Human intelligence. This pressure was imposed in order for leadership to simplify the management of cultures. With this in mind, we see the disruptions as actually having been caused by external dogma, which has tried and failed to satisfy the instinctive needs of mankind housed in the gut intelligence.

The Human needs of Control of individual time and space and of Acceptance of individual behavior in its various environments, is inherent in a more accurate image that we purpose. We see that the problem of Human behavior is to be found in cultures in which external control pressures are imposed and particularly where the animal nature—the instincts—of Humans is denied. The problem is also intensified when the top-down leadership of the culture insists on hanging on to a primitive image of mankind for other purposes than the welfare of the people in that culture.

This issue of subverted control naturally pervades all forms of externally applied control throughout the world where members of the culture have not or cannot establish civil rules against it. It is particularly true when subversion of Human Nature or natural law is involved in an age-old institution that refuses to discard ancient myths. Subverted control and repression of instinctual awareness is prevalent by members in an institution with a refusal to allow logic and thinking—

50

modern sensory data or facts—to be applied in the examination of the truth about the nature of Human beings and Human learning.

You may be aware that very early cultures, prior to conditioning attempts to control both internal and external nature, were more belly centered (see *New Self, New World: Recovering Our Senses in the Twenty-First Century* by Philip Shepherd). But now we have come to a time in Human history in which we must for survival unite body and mind to become more consciously intelligent. It is time that we use both our belly brain (gut feelings) and logical head brain together to evolve into more of what we are designed to be. We find Human beings to be both in need and very close to this extraordinary evolutionary step, due to a developed thinking brain that is now becoming more conscious of innate gut feelings in the body.

The conscious logical awareness of our gut feelings (our second brain) is the final step toward this important unity of body-mind. We have seen in counseling sessions, this transformation begin toward the unity of the two brains in many people (including ourselves) who have experienced the Somatic Reflection Process on gut feelings.

While the dominance of the thinking brain in our modern society (and for many past centuries) has marginalized our awareness of our gut instincts and gut intelligence, we propose that it has been a necessary step in our evolution. For often, Humans swing to one side of a pendulum and then the other, before seeing the need for and being able to unite two attitudes or orientations into one higher intelligence. An example of this in Western history is the prevalence of a past age of feminine culture (more agricultural matriarchal societies, in harmony with nature), also a prevalence of an age of a masculine culture (more hunter-gatherer-city-builder patriarchal societies, with dominance over nature), and now a slow movement toward equality and an integrated feminine-masculine culture (egalitarian). Where past polarities have existed between the head and gut, the new model and awareness of the two brain Human intelligence system, gives us an opportunity to find a higher perspective from which to view life and to have a more balanced position.

Reflections Using Thinking and Feeling in Unity

The ability for Humans to solve problems have been developed ages ago by what were the individual person's external needs, and by what the environments offered up from time to time, disconnected and disjointed, often with the apparent loss of control by the person who was left to guess what's coming next. Fear could overtake any rational planning (thinking), and a feeling in the gut could speak of emptiness and stress. The entire intelligence system, the upper and lower nervous systems, can be in disagreement for an adult to the extent that the person may not be able to find a way out of his or her trauma alone. This situation in our view is the result of the person's unattainable expectation that thinking alone will solve the problems of life. And at the same time, the body is exercising it's power of turning down the levels of energy to get attention to its true needs.

As we reflect on the present struggles and stress facing people in the world—both in the Orient and the Occident—-our thoughts turn to a similar time in the past during the depression of 1929. It was a time of extreme stress and it was very important for a person to have the ability to use both their instincts and logic working together to problem solve. One of the authors writes:

> **My Father lost his job, and then finally lost the family home. This was a devastating blow to my Mother and Father, who had recently left the farm for my father to take a job in a city of industry. They had great expectations for a home of their own, to raise a family, to have a paycheck every week, and to have a car of their own. If it hadn't been for my mother's courage and we two boys with paper routes, and friends, we would have been out in the street. The great expectation of living in the city never returned for my parents. My Father withdrew within himself, and at 52 died in 1943 as we boys went off to war. My Mother died in 1992, three months short of her 100th birthday.**

Of course no one knows what differences existed between the two parents' minds in the head and in the gut. But reflecting on the past dilemma with the present knowledge of Human Nature, we would suggest that his mother had much more conscious and subconscious experience with her combined thinking and feelings than his Father. His Mother had the flexibility to shift her energy to work from inner necessity, as does life, but his father could perceive only the loss of his dream, and it killed him. This is an example of a strong and a weak intuitive system, where the two centers of intelligence of each parent have in one case and have not in the other case had sufficient experience with the head and the gut working together in serious problem-solving.

Looking at time as it is recorded in the brain of the enteric nervous system (in the gut), we find an internal continuity.

53

There we find a history of the past actions taken by the organism—working together whether all those actions were favorable or contrary to the needs of the subject. To find and learn the value of the two centers of intelligence working together, is the building of a useful intuitive process. Such a functioning decision-making process, thinking and feeling applied together (Intuition), not only helps the organism avoid many self-made problems, but also we find it is a major help avoiding stress and aids in navigating our way successfully through problems imposed on us from outside sources. It offers a more positive expectation of the future.

When we reflect on the central nervous system providing sensory information from the outside world, we find sporadic, disjointed, spurious thinking, with only a portion of which is relevant to the needs of the organism. The upper brain is easily distracted by the plethora of exciting offers that tickle the fancies of our senses. The factor that makes this system work for us in the present is the presence of the enteric nervous system, which provides the intuition with feedback of experience of the health related necessities of inner Human Nature.

These necessities of Human Nature define the needs of the species and remind the central nervous system, with its externally focused cognitive brain, of the limits of the many variations it is able to sustain. Without the feedback factor, there would be no Human species, for all the original attempts to build a Human organism without the feedback system between two independent centers of intelligence, (CNS) with its sensory information and (ENS) with its inner and orderly life purpose, could agree on nothing. The upper brain would be chasing after its external fantasy, and there would have been

54

confusion and failure after failure millions of years ago. The awareness of this has depended upon the existence of modern neurological research with its equipment, procedures, methodologies, interests, money, and curiosity, all coming together now to make it possible to look microscopically at what truly has been going on inside the Human gut for ages.

We are now convinced that external rules, laws, doctrines, and dogmas can never control Human behavior for long unless they are in harmony with natural law allowing the instincts to be experienced in the environments into which the newborn is exposed after birth, and continued through the elementary grades.

This conclusion arises from the fact that the child is born without a functioning main brain—without a thinking capacity of its own. It must operate with its instincts alone, its genetic inheritance, and build a main brain from its experiences to cope with its outside environments—a time in life when adults must provide the thinking.

The Mystery of the Instincts and the Young Child

Whatever the child receives in his/her early environments gives the CNS a basic lasting impression of what to expect from its new world—the lasting impact on it from it's early outside world experience—a habit, if you please.

The ability of the child to think for itself must be learned from experience starting at birth in order to exercise Self-control and Self-Acceptance, all with its inner intelligence—the Instincts. It is at birth where the instincts demonstrate the need for attention and it is at birth that the enteric nervous system

(ENS) focuses on the inner satisfaction of the entire organism's energy needs. These two independent systems, when working together can assure the organism that these separate independent functions are in or out of harmony as a unit. Unity between the two is accomplished through a constant dialog between the two systems, which serve as a feedback circuit with needed corrective information from moment to moment—data from the outside world of environments and data from the inside world of energy. The data from the outside is logged in memory of the details of the external happenings, and the data from the Second Brain is logged as feeling experience—the impact on the ENS of the external happening—with totally different points of view.

The functional (useful to the living process) qualities we have sketched are found to be true when there is a conscious effort to seek a balance of the logic of the outside world of the senses with the feelings of the inner world of the body. Both must become dedicated to sustain a balanced life to sustain the species. Fortunately, this balance of thinking and feeling is a learned skill—the Intuition. The child is born with the instincts imbedded in the (ENS) to serve it immediately after birth and throughout life. The thinking becomes imbedded in the central nervous system (CNS) as the senses neurologically develop over years of time with experience. As soon as the conscious use of the instincts matures, it is likely we will find that the time of maturation of the thinking process will follow with its logic.

A short pause of reflection here will reveal how the gamble and the delicacy of this lottery of life has already begun at preconception, and will continue for the remaining years of a lifetime. This could be the prelude to the definition and cultural support of the individual—the recognition that, while we are observed to be different from the outside, we share much more alikeness than difference on the inside.

All of these are necessary tools used by a baby at birth in order for it to find a satisfying future for itself that will continue throughout life, if the environments into which the child is thrust, and the feelings of its instincts are incorporated in the early learning experiences. After all, the child is born without a functioning upper brain and must depend initially on its instincts to find its acceptance in the external world, and learn to control its body to gain Control and Acceptance.

The learning process begins at birth, is tested at puberty, and is completed when the main brain is fully developed, or as long as life exists. We must go all the way back to the beginning of the life-forming process, of conception, to gain an accurate image of what is going on inside the organism, neurologically and genetically, to build the zygote into an organism with the potential to become a fully functioning Human-Being.

Tools of Perception

We ordinarily think of a tool as an object that has been designed for a purpose, a use that will meet our expectations when we learn how to use it to meet an immediate need. We don't often realize that we have used both an expectation of it in our outer world—its shape, form, or characteristics—and the expectation of it for our inner world of satisfaction—what it can do to and for us. In other words, we have formed an image of the tool from experience. We will bring in the simple analogy of a hammer as a tool familiar to everyone to demonstrate what we am reaching for. All hammers have a characteristic designed for pounding. Some hammers have an additional characteristic for pulling nails—a claw hammer.

When we reach for a claw hammer we expect it to pound or remove a nail—it is designed to fulfill a need we have. But because we have little early experience with pounding and removing nails, when we try to hit the nail we miss it and hit the thumb instead. Or when we try to pull a nail with the tool, we also can damage the surface of the wood. The results are that the image of the hammer does not satisfy the need. Not because there was anything wrong with the hammer but because we lacked the experience to use the hammer when needed. We think the point is made——so it is with the gut intelligence of the inner body. The gut intelligence requires previous experience with the main brain in order to function for us when we need it. Experience in life forms images of expectation, and the more experience we have with the use of the image, the sharper and the more accurate the image can become.

The primitive, outdated image of Human Nature to which we have alluded to earlier is one of good and evil, which depends on some outer-world force to maintain control that directs its behavior towards good and minimizes evil. Using the primitive image, the good is dependent on a belief or faith—an assumption that varies from culture to culture—that an external force will minimize intrusions of the instincts from creating the evil. In some faiths the whole body is rejected as the culprit. In the spirit of reality, this is a feeling from external observations that this force has an anthropomorphic quality, which returns favors for good behavior for the faith and punishment for the evil. Acceptance for the faith and good behavior could be rewarded by a better life to come hereafter—after death. Both faith and belief can degenerate into control of the believer by external earthly forces, using faith to shield the corruption, with little or no regard for Human Nature. History is full of examples of corruption of Natural Law, which work until they are ultimately destroyed by the energy of natural law—the nature of we animals.

The Inside World of Humankind

The idea that the Human has two centers of intelligence, not just one in the head but also one in the gut, is unthinkable for many people at first. As we began to examine Dr. Michael Gershon's medical breakthrough in 1998 and his finding that Humans have two distinct independent nervous systems and what this could mean to Human behavior, we perceived that the nature of the feed-back link between the two independent systems would give the organism greater control to think, feel, and act. If the two centers are cooperating towards the same objective—maintaining life's needs—and in constant communication with each other, then such a system has the ability and purpose to establish a complex communication system that could control the organism's own behavior, without some interfering external power. With the growing main brain intimately nestled around the animal brain in the skull, this electro-chemical arrangement in animals suggests that such a system of communication is what has evolved within them over time. It has probably increased animal longevity based on need and demand for many species.

A Human control system located external to the Human organism is subject to the whims and fancies for all manner of purposes, and has long been the subject of corruption of power over minds of men. From the eighth Century, when Charlemagne; (Charles 1), emperor of the West (800-814 AD); established the Holy Roman Empire, by a questionable process of his conversion to Christianity or by force—the choice depends on which side of his movement you wish to take. His movement has had a major political affect on the cultures of the Orient and the Occident—Eastern and Western civilization, characterized by exercising control of Human minds away from the use of Human instincts of body intelligence in social intercourse.

Charlemagne, in the eighth century was, by no means, the first to recognize the value of Human mind control for power over his subjects. As early as the second century, Bishops throughout Europe and the Middle East were busy defending the 'pure faith', which reportedly came directly from the Apostles by word of mouth. Many others had their own ideas of what was and was not Christian thought and behavior.

> Joseph Campbell, in the 20th century is reputed to have said about faith:
>
> "I don't have to have faith, I have experience."

It has taken us a while to understand the meaning of Campbell's simple statement, for at first it seems to be a judgment against believing in anything. We think Campbell is saying that Human experience allows for change to be expected of life and we can cultivate the adaptability to meet these challenges of change as they occur. Faith tends to fix expectation in time, and fails to prepare Humans with the tools to cope with inevitable change. Expectation is a tool, which at its best, directs our attention into the future. Faith is not a functional tool, when a culture tries to transplant past-comfort into the future while ignoring the changes that have occurred all around them.

These dynamics of illogical faith reflects our awareness back to the statement of John Kennedy: "… we enjoy the comfort of opinion without the discomfort of thought." We raise this issue because it is a fundamental principal that may help point the direction to our cultural leadership and certainly to the education dilemma we face in this culture and in other cultures around the world.

We are now able to perceive the past with a different perspective, of which our predecessors were denied by being born too soon. We now can not only observe Human behavior as they did, but we can now find the meaning of the behavior. Human behavior is designed to often learn what a person needs to know about herself or himself, not to satisfy the observer's miss-judgment—often subconsciously. There is no doubt in our minds that our predecessors experienced their gut feelings, as we do. They did so without knowing that as they took the freedom to think for themselves, they were exercising their intuitive intelligence against the prevailing external controls. Every other person in the world is in our outside world, and to "me", there is only one inside world that is "mine" to protect. We may even be a twin but the impact on us of our experience in life is our difference—our treasure—our individuality.

Our Inner Human Needs

We have 'bundled' the two instinctual needs, the inner necessities, into two general needs in our new Human image; they are: 1. the need of Self-Control (the freedom to respond naturally and authentically), and 2. The need of Self-Acceptance (attention from other members of the Human family). One necessity of Human Nature, which brings the need for attention into balance, is the need to be in charge of our own space and time, in our own lives. If not freely given, nature provides the energy and the will to seize control, or die for that natural right. The control side of balanced-necessity, along with acceptance, provides Human Nature with the learned possibility of caring for themselves and for other's personal and social lives.

We have a simple way of explaining the necessity of this balance—it is like a child's teeter/totter. If you take too much control in Human relationships, others may loose interest in you, pay you less attention or distrust you and reject you. If you give others, too much attention, others may take over and try to control your time and space—your life. The dynamics of this ditty reflects the constant struggle for a delicate balance of these neurological needs (refer back to diagrams in chapter 2).

In 2007, using research at the Max Plank Institute for Human Development in Berlin, Gerd Gigerenzer made a major contribution in the field of Psychology and the understanding of Human Nature. In his book *Gut Feelings: The Intelligence of the Unconscious*, he depicts Human Nature as caring for each other due to our instinctual social need for belonging and protecting both family and community. He also opened the door for the exploration of intuition and gut feelings as an evolutionary response. It is his positive view of humankind that Gigerenzer should be applauded for, as it flies in the face of traditional psychological thought by giants such as Freud who viewed humankind as driven by more "selfish" motivations.

Social Psychologists have since taken up where Gigerenzer left off on the subject of Human social needs. In *Social: Why Our Brains Are Wired to Connect*, Social Psychologist Matthew Lieberman expands further details of neurological studies (including his own) on the subject of human social instincts and our need for social networks driving our evolution and behaviors, as well as being at the core of our Human Nature. He concludes quite convincingly that *being social* is a basic human need.

Interestingly, Lieberman presents the idea that our more social psychological needs are actually more important to satisfy first than our biological needs, with the biological needs depending on the satisfying of the most basic social need first. His example of this inverts Maslow's *Hierarchy of Needs* and suggests that the most fundamental human need for the helpless newborn infant is social connection, first needing a mother/caregiver to help him/her satisfy basic biological needs (mother's presence is primary to feeding).

If we acknowledge this innate need to be socially connected, Lieberman suggests that we could be headed as a species in a positive and more successful manner, and this is particularly important in education of our children. We relate this need to be social to our findings that Humans have as one of two instinctual needs felt in the gut response of emptiness and fullness, the need for acceptance from others (attention).

Following Your Truth

David Cawood, University of British Columbia professor and author of a recent ground-breaking book in change management and executive development titled *The Secret Sabbatical,* reminds us that one's truth is only possible to know after self-reflection on a deep level in the unconscious in which we are allowed to recover our imagination and thus discover our true destiny. He describes this as "not a quick fix" but inner work that takes effort and time. Our experience in counseling has been that a new perception of self and others is resulted only by using both centers of intelligence—gut and head brains—to discover one's inner instinctual needs of acceptance (attention) and control (freedom). For most adults, this is a process that takes time reflecting somatically back on gut feelings in early childhood to update our awareness of self.

If we on a daily bases utilize our intuition to deal with life's issues, we have to consciously both think and feel. If we both think and feel consciously, then we will see new possibilities. If we perceive new possibilities that meet our needs, we need to act. When we act, we need energy. When the feeling of energy is strongest, that is the truth, the choice for us! With this new set of tools, we can fill life's emptiness with fullness of need, and energy to cope.

> "If you follow your bliss, you put yourself on a kind of track that has been there all the while, waiting for you, and life that you ought to be living is the one you are living."
>
> —Joseph Campbell from *The Power of Myth*

The Nature of Learning

This chapter further expands our understanding of the Human learning process and demonstrates how Humans "copy" from nature rather than "invent" all the systems of our modern life, including systems of technology. With this in mind, more is explained about the importance of and how Humans (in order to survive and not self-destroy) must begin to expand our awareness of our Human Nature and gut instincts and apply it to the systems we "invent" in our modern culture. We also further explain the importance of experience in the learning process, with our instincts as the energy source for all of life's activities.

Technology and nature both begin with a primitive model where there are separate functions to be coordinated into a single unit through the use of feedback. Over time they can be developed into a highly sophisticated, stable system. We Humans simply copy——consciously or subconsciously—— nature's intelligence, and add this intelligence to the curious, intuitive, minds of ordinary Human beings. You may quickly understand this process of copying nature if you reflect on how the first wheel may well have been first thought of after a Human being watched a snow ball roll down a hill.

Nature's Systems and Human Systems

We think that some reflections on a few common technological discoveries will support this point that man-made systems are developed as a copy of nature's systems:

The Airplane: About 500 years ago, Leonardo da Vinci copied birds in flight when he drew his famous sketches of flying machines. After centuries of other's attempts to fly, Wilbur and Orville Wight were the first to fly a powered aircraft.—all inspired by the flight of birds.

The Steam Engine: Thomas Savery: In 1698, he boiled water and harnessed it for pumping water from mines.

Electricity: Ben Franklin: Flying a kite in a storm, lightening hit his kite and knocked him to the ground.

The Telephone: Alexander Graham Bell and Elisha Gray: Both developed a device that could transmit speech by electricity. Bell, copying nature's ability to solve the problem of hearing (the Human ear), invented a kind of electromechanical ear in 1875, in which a person could speak into a tube with a membrane that resembled the eardrum and amplified the vibrations of speech the same way as the bones of the middle ear.

The Automobile: In 1672, Ferdinand Verbiest built the first steam-powered vehicle as a toy for the Chinese Emperor.

Bionics: Along with the obvious robotics that copies living organisms, Velcro is a modern example of bionics that was inspired by burrs from the burdock plant. Now scientist are working on bulletproof vests spun from artificial spider web filaments.

Fractals: They are used in modern computing in graphic arts programs and video games to model structures. They are complex patterns through repetition, with Benoit Mandelbrot given the credit for popularizing fractal geometry in 1980. Iterating patterns multiple times, fractal geometry can model the natural phenomena. In nature, fractals can be observed in trees, human body blood vessels, crystal growth patterns and wind.

And the list of man-made copies of nature goes on and on......

It is useful to look at the functionality of the Sciences we have discovered, borrowed, copied, found, or intuited the intelligence from within our Selves. We have actually invented nothing but have developed a special intuitive intelligence from our own experiences of problem solving as we grew to maturity, observed, and interacted with the natural world around us. From this observation, we can project that advancements in scientific discoveries are directly related to how in tune we become with our inner nature.

The difference between nature's systems and those of Humans is: nature's systems are based on necessary components of life on earth, stabilizing the form of energy it uses with no waste of energy, whereas man-made copies of nature's systems may have no value to Human Nature at all—they may even be destructive to Human Nature. To assure that our human copies (technological "inventions" and anything man-made) are beneficial to the Human species, we Humans need a broader understanding of our needs, and the value of need satisfaction to the preparation for Human intelligence. This calls for personal experience as an important component of the process of learning about the Human Self.

The key to primitive-system discoveries and development is that there is always a necessary feedback circuit sending sensory information back to the input—whether internally or externally applied. Without this active channel of constant

67

communications and feedback connection in both nature's and man made systems, systems discoveries are unstable—they can spin out of control and destroy themselves. We cannot afford to continue to neglect the inner needs of Human life, less over time we become one of nature's experimental-recycled failures.

Instincts as Tools For Learning

The intuition is based on past stored intelligence, which requires a combination of sensory experience and feeling experience. The newborn, having no experience of its own, will have to use its instincts at birth, and copy what it learns from its external environment over time as the senses develop. These timely experiences will determine its stored intelligence (CNS), which when working with the available animal brain (ENS) will be used in its future life for learning and solving problems. So the quality of life will be dependent upon the decisions it makes with the intelligence available from the two centers. The more diverse the experience, the more useful to the organism the results become.

The tools for learning at birth are built into the Human organism as *Instincts*. These instincts are designed to find the source of nourishment and intimate contact with its immediate caretaker—its mother. The infant has had some experience with its senses of her smell, touch, and taste while in the womb. The logic of this design provides intimate contact with the source of food—the instincts designed in the mother just for this occasion. Sight and sound complete the tools for more distant use by the organism's will, when developed over time, and become the tools of additional protection and safety. As the organism becomes mobile, this tool-kit becomes the

68

functional Central Nervous System (CNS), focused on the outside world storing and sending information of its experience in its external environments to the Enteric Nervous System (ENS) in the gut.

Since the ENS was built and running at birth, the development of the CNS functionality establishes the feedback link between the two centers of intelligence, and the learning process for the organism has begun. The CNS provides the thinking and physical skill intelligence and the ENS provides the feeling—the necessities and satisfactions of life. Both of these centers of intelligence are essential for the growth of Human intelligence in a truly healthy and functioning capacity.

In approaching the idea of the process of learning, we need to bring into the awareness the essential, dual functions of Control and Acceptance (Freedom and Attention). We also need to understand that the ENS can operate independent of CNS at will (see *The Second Brain*). This independence accommodates the presence of several semi-independent vital functions for the CNS and the ENS to cooperate with chewing and swallowing and rejection of food, if not acceptable. If the excrement is not of the proper texture, it can be held voluntarily by the CNS, or rejected by the ENS. Breathing rate can be increased by the CNS from external sensory stimulation or decreased by the ENS when the stomach is full.

Then there is the matter of energy!

The Energy Generator

If we can think in terms of energy for a moment, the food in the digestive tract is the energy source, the fuel for the generator, which provides the energy used throughout the body, and the enteric nervous system is part of the distribution network that circulates that energy to every part of the body, even to the upper brain. These two autonomic functions, the generation and distribution of energy, are essential to all life processes. These two vital functions, which are at the center of the inner body, keep the entire Human life systems operating regardless of what is happening outside the organism or what the upper brain is doing—thinking, sensing, remembering, sleeping or dying, etc. On the other hand, whatever the main upper brain is engaged in, affects the gut. The sensory data from the upper brain is either in support of or in conflict with the energy source.

The Gut as the Individual's Creator

A new experience can be an impulsive expectation into the future in prospect, based on data or information we previously acquired from past experience. In our very early childhood, there is not much stored information with which to think—not much intelligence with which to guide it. Therefore, *trial and learn* over time is our key to successful experience. We have a necessity to learn how to achieve our individual objectives in life from the inside world of satisfaction. It takes time to make mistakes and correct them, therefore, human history has a very slow evolutionary learning curve.

> "Experience is a hard teacher because she gives the test first, the lesson afterwards."
> —Vern Law, Picher for American Major League Baseball (MLB) for the Pittsburgh Pirates

At conception a process begins, which will use the Mother's Womb, the lucky Genes, the DNA/RNA—Nature's Designer/Builder—the energy of Nature's electro-chemistry and the elemental materials required in the structural design. From this assembly of 'materials', design objectives, and a Mother's internal care, there normally emerges nature's individual example of life—a potential Human life in every cell of the body. It is still an unfinished product, for it will take time for the Enteric Nervous System (ENS) to continue to cautiously help with the completion of the main brain structure and its Central Nervous System (CNS), to complete the creation of the Human.

The Importance of Experience

The importance of experience is universally known in every action we take in life, and is an essential aspect of learning. The use of the ancient image—the image of Human's need for an external source of control of our good and evil behavior—simply does not fill Human needs. The evidence of the history of Human behavior with this Greco-Roman image has been copied by almost every established culture on the face of the earth. This action is excusable in the past, since medical science and experience has only discovered this more accurate multiple-brains image in the last fifteen years.

On the other hand, the inadequate primitive image of how Humans function has been experienced for at least two thousand years, and is by now buried deep in the Human psyche as what is believed the truth about an external God and salvation in the hereafter. The radical change to a two-brain Human image of self-control and self-regulation certainly is a difficult understanding of oneself for many people as it requires a change from viewing the idea of having only a God external (conceptualized by our thinking head brain) to the awareness of divine energy within us (related to the feeling gut brain) and self-regulation. We take this idea up more thoroughly in our unit on instincts and religion.

Upheaval of cultures, where Human energy is missing its freedom and acceptance, is ripe for change from a negative environment of denial to an environment of self-control and acceptance. Still this change is difficult and takes time. We see this today in these examples of denial:

*Only some have accepted the idea of climate change in the face of plenty of experience and scientific evidence. This lack of public support of the need for alternative energy has allowed the suppression of scientific inventions and discovery of important alternatives sources in favor of a fossil fuel economy (i.e., the suppression of Nikola Tesla alternating of current technologies, fluorescent tubes, radar, and bladeless turbines, as well as the suppression claims of many modern inventors of new energy sources like cell battery energy and water-to-energy electrolysis process).

*Only some have accepted the humanitarian direction and cooperative management of our economic and political systems—we are having this struggle at present in the United States.

*Only some may be able to accept efforts to make radical changes in our public education system without some experimental evidence.

The possibility of an intelligent consensus will be achieved only when we can base decision-making on what is needed for the sake of our Human Nature. The perverted idea that external solutions can be found on the basis of power, prestige, and money, omits the fact that Nature—Human Nature—is the ultimate source of power, and we had better not forget it.

Conclusions: Ideal Learning

Ideal learning requires a clear mind for Human Beings with a sensory awareness of its responsibility to the life processes in the body, with which it is born. The clear mind is dependent upon the early environmental quality in which the organism finds itself. If a supportive environment is missing, in order to correct any damage that has occurred, the person will need to learn to reflect with his/her own feeling on the past negative experiences. Then with help, he/she will thoughtfully erase the negative impact on its Self Image. We developed the Somatic Reflection Process (SRP) for that specific purpose. If a child is fortunate enough to find its environment supportive of its life processes and its experience with self-control and self-acceptance, then it will grow, and its experience will remain intact with an added expectation for further positive experiences.

The goal of this learning process is to develop a culture of curious individual minds, creative and independent thinkers, intuitionally intelligent people who are caring for each other and have a habit of wanting to learn more about themselves and others in the world.

We look forward to a time when we can experience more cooperation and less competition in all cultures; when prestige, power, and wealth for the few will be recognized as an

73

indication of an empty life; when all lives are valued more than things; when money provides basic necessity; when societies learn how to coordinate inner intelligence with external intelligence as we take small steps into the future; and when intelligent experience, and a "Reverence for Life" as Albert Schweitzer's suggests, abounds in all individuals.

Evolving Communal Mind

We have examined how Humans copy rather than invent, all from our interactions with the natural world. We also propose that we invent/copy from our own inner instinctive needs fulfillment. The following is an exploration of how our instinctual needs for freedom and acceptance have propelled Humans to invent our modern technological society with cell phones, the world wide web, and social networking that spans the global community. Even more interestingly, we look at where this is taking us in our future and how our Human species could be just at the beginning of working toward developing telepathic abilities and increasing our intuition, all to satisfy our Human instinctual needs.

We may hear some people complain that our propensity toward using social networking and cell phones, particularly when we are in a public or social situation, are signs that we modern Humans are a bunch of disassociated people who don't know how to sit in the same room together and relate to each other anymore. But wouldn't it be a calming thought to think of this behavior as also being indicative of a new Human skill we are fervently developing through the use of such devices—the ability to bond with others from a distance—as taking baby steps toward telepathy and Intuitional Intelligence that could bring us all even closer together than we currently imagine. Let's explore this!

Just a couple of weeks ago, we happened on a discussion on our Facebook feed among some "friends"—one of which is a prominent author—who were all rather puzzled at the fact that they had so many feelings for "internet friends" they had known for a couple of years but never actually met in person. They were writing that they felt sad with a heavy feeling of loss because one of them had deceased. It was a virtual communication cluster of Humans who had never met in physical form but were sharing an actual experience of mourning, grief, and were comforting each other over the loss of another someone they also had never met in physical form. Something very important around bonding from a distance had been learned by these friends. As far as social scientists know or have recorded, this type of skill in relating with intimacy from a distance is a fairly new species behavior in modern Human history that is growing globally in occurrence with our advances in telecommunications and social networking. To social scientists like ourselves, it is worthy of noting and speculating upon where it could take our species and how it could affect our Human condition.

If we are learning that we do not need to be in the same locality together, that we do not need a close proximity and physical relationship in order to feel close and to share thoughts and feelings, to comfort each other emotionally and feel intimate in that sense, and to feel accepted by and care for each other, then is this fundamentally changing us and our psychological competencies and functions as Human beings? Of course it most likely is, even if it is a very slow, almost unrecognizable, transformation of our species. So perhaps we can speculate where it is taking us in the long run and just relax and enjoy the ride.

We could speculate that the internet and cell phones are our training wheels for learning to connect to the Noosophere and then develop telepathy in the further future as a species. And if so, will we one day develop telepathy through the use of something kin to implantable cell phones and/or eventually make structural adaptations more naturally by learning to use our higher faculties that are already within our potential consciousness? Neuroscientist Miguel Nicolelis of Duke University has announced that his lab has created in rats the first brain-to-brain internet communication called "organic" computing as a precursor to telepathy (he also professes that computers will never replicate the human brain because the human brain is not computable). The potential of this discovery may all sound undesirable to us now, cell phones in our heads, and the idea that with telepathy we could be so transparent that people know everything that we think and feel. But many of us remember also when the idea of just having a cell phone seemed horrid—the idea that by carrying a phone around and giving people the opportunity to call you anytime anywhere you went, felt like a completely unwanted invasion of privacy.

To explore these questions of our telepathic future, we first need to look at how telepathy could be a progressive necessity

76

for us as a species and what value it would have to us psychologically. It would surely alter the nature of Human interactions and relationships as we know it today and, in fact, the leanings we have toward becoming telepathic appear to already be doing so.

Many of our families of origin have spread themselves all over the globe with a common scenario of grandma in Ohio and her children in Seattle, Tampa, and Houston, with her grandchildren now in Bangkok, New York City and Hawaii. We have scattered our seeds and diversified, stepping into new environments spread wide apart, surrounding the globe. We now have so much to hold together in relationships and it is so much work to stay connected as a family of origin, to keep in communication. Many people have found that they needed to diversify their families and adopt more local extended family members in order to have an immediate community to fill the Human need for intimacy. And some of our adopted, extended family members are not local but are ones we have never actually meet in the flesh, only in virtual time through social networking.

We know through science that nature in its workings, including our Human Nature, is conservative, and it does not waste energy. Nature does not try an experiment or make a change in a species without a necessity or survival reason for an adaptation and without an underlying principle to follow. As we have explained in previous chapters, it has been our life work in psychology and education to explore the intelligence of our Human Nature, and in doing so we have discovered that we Human beings have two instinctual needs—acceptance (intimacy, attention, security and containment) and freedom (control of our own responses to life) that we strive to keep them in balance from moment-to-moment.

If we accept that we have an innate striving towards the balance for our needs of acceptance and freedom, then we can view this new skill in bonding and intimacy at a distance as an attempt of our nature to bring ourselves into balance of these two needs. Working off this theory of inner needs, it seems logical that we would have reason and motive to learn telepathic skills as an adaptation to the isolation of the social environment we have created, with families spread out in distance around the globe. Telepathy would undoubtedly increase our communications and intimacy with others and be one way we could balance our need for acceptance with the vast freedoms we have already taken or find necessary in the future to take as a species in even further reaches interstellar.

Throughout history, a species, plant or animal life, will assure its continued existence and arrest its very extinction by biologically diversifying and by adaptation to the changing environment in which it inhabits. Seeds cast themselves into the wind to spread and diversify and must adapt to sometimes hitherto uninhabited territories. This causes necessary changes in the species. If you accept science, then the history of Humankind shows we are no different than other animals in this adaptation process (although note that both our reasoning ability and spirituality distinguishes us), as we are not the same Humans in our biological functioning abilities that we were thousands of years ago. Even if you agree with those scientists who view Humans and Neanderthals as possibly two separate species, you can see that Humans have adapted and changed in their communication skills and consciousness through the ages. Taking into account the need for this adaptation process,

78

it is perhaps then no accident that we have created and embraced technology on all fronts to include the ensuring of the accessibility of international air travel and the use of computers and telephones to a point that we have widened our worldview to include all people as our intimate community. And we are still working on widening this worldview to include a more complete global consciousness.

Perhaps the growth of becoming more telepathic as a species is a necessary tool to help us break down the communication barriers on the path to our real Human destiny of truly becoming conscious of the fact that we are one Human Family.

For now we leave this subject for you to think on, but then if we are asking these questions then maybe the communal mind or Noosophere has communicated through the global electromagnetic field and you too are already pondering these possibilities.

The Second Brain Affects Upon Self Awareness and Human Development

In the following chapter, we explore what the definition is of the true Self and what it means when applied to the understanding that Humans have two functional brains, rather than just one.

The Self has been a nebulous mystery and remains so until we become aware that it expresses a concept of the Human spirit and the idea that this spirit is within all creatures and has independent energy of consciousness and action—the energy of life itself, which disappears only when life is terminated.

Let us first briefly recap what we already know about the Enteric Nervous System (ENS) and the Central Nervous System (CNS). The Second Brain, sitting on top of the spinal column in the skull cavity, is connected to the ENS through the spinal cord, and its sensors are primarily distributed throughout the inner body of the digestive process in the gut. The Main Brain is connected to the CNS, and its sensors are spread primarily throughout the entire external body. Each system has its own functional responsibility to the continued life of the organism. The Main Brain with its senses, (sight, sound, taste, touch, and smell), is focused on the organism's well-being in its external environment and must also cooperate with the ENS where they interface.

The external points of interface are located where food enters the body, which requires the transfer of food to be carefully selected and introduced by the CNS and to be accepted by the mouth by the ENS or to be regurgitated. Where the waste leaves the body, under normal conditions of digestion, control by either system can conveniently take over. Internal cooperation exists between the two systems relative to the heart and lungs. There is a constant two-way contact between the two systems—much like the purpose of the communication system used in a ship, where the helmsman has an essential two-way contact with the engine room to report what is going on in the ship's external environment. At the same time, the engineer in the engine room must at a moments notice furnish the necessary energy to meet the demand to instantly maneuver the ship. The two-way neurological systems of life are operating at even a higher speed—at millisecond speed—to meet demands.

When we as Humans design operating systems, they require a feed back link with Human intelligence connected with the direct energy source—for instance steam power, a battery, an electric motor, or direct sunlight, etc—in order for the system to be stable. This Human feed back link is also necessary to keep the energy source in control from destroying itself. With the development of the electronic control systems, which allows for fixed automatic control, there is still required a Human intelligence to program the system.

The life system, which nature provides for we Humans at birth, is a completely closed energy system (ENS). It receives its power from indirect use of the sun for its source of food. The intelligence of ENS, and that of the animal brain, is the energy and intelligence that we possess to design and build us. It has the ability to guide and sustain us throughout life.

Definition of the True Self

Let's for a minute start with the functionality of the experienced Human adult's intelligence and work backward to determine what is the definition of the true Self. And let us see what, if any, current meaning the true Self has with the concept of two brains, rather than just one. The new dynamic model of Human Nature demands a more accurate image of how we function for medical practitioners, psychiatrists, psychologists, and individuals to effectively interpret the dynamics of Human behavior. Medical science research is providing the neurological aspects of this image. And as we have pointed out, we are providing the conversion of the medical perspective to a psycho-behavioral perspective of the new image. Our experience has discovered the Human need for the new image in all Human activity.

We have already defined the Human organism as a closed system, and is a group of electro-chemical components, or other internal similar systems, which are capable of producing and sustaining life—a mobile Human organism. Each component functions in such a manner as to create, sustain, and perpetuate an intelligence system——the mobile Human organism. Like all of nature's systems, the Enteric Nervous System (ENS) derives its energy from nature, from sources available indirectly from the Sun. The form of energy that the organism needs is then converted to electro-chemistry by its own generator——the Human digestive system. The Human digestive system provides the elements of each organ's requirements by participating in the circulation of nutrients throughout the body. This function depends on the various organs to use the electrochemical conversions of the nutrients in the blood to take care of it own inherent needs. Each organ has a pathway for waste products. The air products are exchanged: oxygen is separated out for purification of the blood and carbon dioxide is exhaled for use by vegetation in a system of conservation. The digestion-system eliminates waste products, for solids have a direct path to the anus. Liquid waste products find osmotic paths to the urinary tract and to the bladder. Then both waste products are excreted back to nature for reuse—nothing truly wasted over time!

The ENS is the life center of the Human organism. Its composition is from the parental gene pool, with those genes available in the individual's male parent's sperm, which performs the internal process of fertilization of the female parent's egg. Under normal conditions this process provides the beginning of Life, and will provide all of the necessary intelligence needed by birth time. The plan to finish the mobile Human Being is within the same fertilized mothers egg, and includes the instructions to finish the electrochemical and neurological development of the sensory brain in the skull with its central nervous system (CNS) distributed throughout the body. All of these sensors are scattered throughout the entire body, where they are needed to facilitate communications between the two systems.

Gambles of Life

We will inject a bit of philosophy at this point to raise an issue, which in youth is most often in the subconscious, then begins to emerge to a conscious level at mid-life. The two brain image has a way of facing us with a new understanding of our individuality, a new nature of our Selves. If you reflect on the previous paragraphs about the beginning of the Human organism, we think you will agree with us that life is one gamble after another.

It is fortuitous that our particular parents found each other. It is again fortuitous for each of us to receive an unknown set of genes from them. We are lucky if the genes we receive from them are healthy and produce a well-formed zygote. Then if we are lucky, we will have a normal birthing experience, and land in a stabile environment, which fills our needs of complete acceptance and loving care immediately at birth. The experiences in our environments, without the use of the ENS later, will not fill our needs of a full life after birth.

If we also develop and maintain an awareness of the life processes of the ENS (the life center along with the development of the CNS), then the center of cognition (which can act as a needs satisfaction reference to the self) increases the odds for a full life. If we are not given the chance early in life to cultivate this relationship between the two centers, the CNS and ENS, we will find that our decision-making will not be significantly improved with age, and our accuracy will become associated with the chaos of the outside world. And in that case, the accuracy of our decisions as adults—making decisions without a conscious use of the ENS—will be by chance. And if we are not good at guessing, then we will likely produce empty life experiences as we age. With a consciously integrated CNS and ENS, the odds in making life decisions, with some luck, will begin to approach a satisfying full life.

An additional aspect of a full life is that following an integrated pattern from early childhood experience promotes a curious habit of having interest in others. This life path of fullness leads our own experiences to sponsor a more diverse understanding of ourselves, a desire to care more about the fullness or emptiness of the life experiences of others, and more caring for others. When we become more caring of other's needs, we tend to sponsor more intimate and self-controlled relationships of everyone we encounter.

A Metaphor of Human Experience

We offer this metaphoric image of human experience that came to us in one of our discussions long ago about the true Self:

(ME) represents my *CNS*, my persona, which is my intelligence gathered from my external world alone in my environments over time. It is my name, my position, my status in the world, my image of myself, my language—everything others sense of my external qualities. Problem solving with *(ME)* alone is full of purely guesswork, and if used alone my life will be stressed with emptiness.

(MY SELF) represents my *ENS*, my life support system, my species, and my inner private world of my own. It is my Feeling center, my Energy, and my support from its unique intelligence. It represents pure Feeling. With the Somatic Reflection Process (SRP*)*, we can center on this pure feeling in the gut to discover the traumatic impacts of the past and to bring disturbing issues to the present to help a person to solve.

(I) represents my integrated Self, my *CNS* and *ENS* working together seeking a full life with others. It is my combined intelligence from the environmental impacts on my life. Problem solving with *(I)* in any environment, will raise the accuracy of life's problem solutions, reflectively developing the practice as a habit, setting a path toward the life I was designed to live, and I can become my True Self with time and practice.

Protection of the Integrated Self

The present understanding and use of the single brain image of Human Nature adds considerable difficulty to the application of ENS coordinated with the CNS when dealing with others.

This problem is, in part, due to the lack of experience with the use of these two systems simultaneously. It takes some time and effort to reflect, to examine the impact on the life center ENS in the gut to reach the independent feelings.

The effort for any recent disturbing happenings provides information recorded in the gut, which has content relative to the individual life——personal design—and it will encourage habitual use of an integrated Self. The result will be relief from stress, from ones own guilt from the past incident, from uncontrollable hostility towards another, and from fear of damage to a valued relationship in the future. You will find this effort will also save a significant quantity of energy.

Apologetics

We are cautiously aware of present acceptance of the dogma that has permeated thinking around the world in almost every activity of Human existence, some of which is the result of a lack of tools to be used to explore the powerful abilities of inner Human Nature. However, much is dedicated to the power of universal personal gain of one type or another that has been applied and spread for centuries since the emergence of the Roman Catholic Church—for at least thirteen centuries.

The dogma of the eighth century contains a notion that independent thinkers should not be allowed membership in the emerging Church. As we have previously expressed, remnants of that doctrine still exist professing that Human Nature requires an external power to control it of its capacity to demonstrate good and evil actions. This need for external control is generally inaccurately hailed, as we have pointed out, due to what is commonly thought of as the unreliability of

Human instincts. This idea had an alternative purpose, which was and is an ideal way to use as a powerful instrument for Human mind control, and this may well have been the primary objective at its genesis. In any case, the dogma became the foundation of Human behavior control in all Mid Eastern and Western Cultures—perhaps now, all over the World.

When we used the Somatic Reflection Process with students on the college level to reflect upon their feelings and review the early period of their lives—a time in their lives where it was simple and the impact of *trial and learn* was without a mature thinking upper Brain, the person would find that cultural standards had been imposed as a negative judgment upon them as early as their memory served them (usually at three or four years old). This standard or judgment had periodically imposed itself on the consciousness of the person up until their present life. The student would rarely speak out in the group and express their feelings in cases where severe negative judgments had occurred upon the person for having taken needed instinctual, simple, curious, learning, actions of early childhood and beyond. However in a response paper, which was required for a grade at the end of the course, they would often write about their feelings or request private sessions to discuss their problems.

With this understanding from the students, we searched our own feelings together finding the same judgments that the students expressed, and we experienced the same impact on our instincts and the same blocks to being conscious of our true inner self.

We also found that the critical years of this damage were often during puberty, where that period rendered the greatest confusion and damage to a person's sexuality. We then spent

87

hours searching for the source of the judgments, and found that the basic truth rested squarely on the laws of a culture—religious law and its underlying structure of civil law. We were searching for the truth for cultural standards of behavior. We concluded that there were powerful conflicts between man-made laws (religious and civil), and the natural laws of the universe—with which we are intimately connected, with which we are driven, and of which we need to be aware and accept in order to survive as the Human species. Remember that the gut brain is the only brain completely developed at birth and the thinking brain continues to develop after birth until it is whole. With the denial of our gut brain or feeling brain, we are without the ability to defend our Selves from thoughtless negative judgments of others and the culture.

Part 2

Instinctual Awareness and It's Affects Upon Longevity

Aging With Instinctual Awareness

This essay explores Human Nature and how we might best use our instincts to prepare for the aging process that begins at birth and for increasing longevity into our elder years. Not surprisingly, being aware of your instinctual gut feelings not only increases your Intuitional Intelligence but also has positive affects upon longevity.

The present knowledge of the functional qualities of Human life is based on reflective experience in psychology and the research of neurobiologists. These combined efforts have provided science with a more accurate knowledge of the functionality of the internal gut. Science also provides an insight of a new functional image capable of providing Human Nature with greater control of the self—a breakthrough for the health and intelligence of Humans. Focusing attention on Human aging is a task-in-progress, since we presently can re-examine the functionality of the aging process with the same Human two-brain-image we used to understand the intelligence that we now know supports life. We do not think this effort is meaningless, for learning with the two-brain-image has exposed possibilities that the single brain Human image could not provide.

There are two very important discoveries that come from the knowledge that we can offer:

1. **The first one, and we have discussed this in length already, is total freedom of the instinctual and functional qualities of the animal brain with its Enteric Nervous System (ENS)—the instincts toward obtaining a balance of the need for acceptance and for control (freedom).**

2. **And the second one is the Somatic Reflection Process (SRP) that we offer as a valuable tool when needed to dislodge and eliminate past trauma through gut feeling awareness.**

Human traumas (however large or small) are often based on experiences in which our expectations of control or acceptance were over-looked by an innocent member of the family. Feelings of guilt, hostility or fear, for which a child will assume responsibility early in life, often impact the enteric nervous system years before the thinking CNS (logic) can moderate the trauma. Such an experience can grow into a major stress that—like a bad tooth—needs to be removed. We know that using the Somatic Reflection Process will reduce stress from these traumas, which are the cause of much discomfort and disease of the digestive system, and possibly elsewhere in our lives, at all ages. We also feel assured of new insights from our own experience with aging (we are 96 and 68 years old) as we embark on this extension of our life's study.

The individuality—what we learn about our selves from the outside world—is the result of the impact of our experience in the environments in which we were born and raised. It is at this early time in our lives when we are the most vulnerable, when we are introduced to the outside world, with only our instincts to guide our movements, sounds, reactions, responses. This is also the time in our life that the culture, in which we are born, can inform us of who we are in the outside world, and begin to show us our external differences. Without the presence of the animal brain with its enteric nervous system—its Human instincts, its DNA, RNA, and its experience—there would be no Human Life as we know it, no consistent species. So as we turn to the process of aging, we can anticipate some interesting surprises.

We have spent time discussing the learning process, and the functionality of the two main brain systems that serve the Human animal throughout its life span—its struggle to come into life and its struggle to maintain its self in life. Understanding these two main brain systems of intelligence as one unit working together is necessary to produce life in the Human organism that can bring health and satisfaction and serve up self-controlled behavior in the learning process of a child. Once the qualities of self-control and self-acceptance are learned as habits in childhood—as most of our behavior is learned—we can look forward to respectful, self-managed individuals throughout a lifetime.

Preparing for Longevity

We have spent most of our lives in school learning, and we have seldom encountered education preparation or courses for having a long meaningful satisfaction with life, nor the subject of longevity, a long duration of life. We find this subject of longevity most important to study, perhaps more so when we view wellness and happiness of Human life in the now as an ultimate goal.

Medical research and psychological experience in the late 20th Century discovered much about the functional processes that have maintained life inside the Human animal body for ages. From that research and experience, science has discovered the combined value of a sensory brain and an animal brain as they function together to produce human intelligence capable of managing its own behavior. By concentrating attention on the animal brain in the gut, while the sensory brain gradually begins to assume its function of protection of the life center, we can begin to develop a habit of awareness of the satisfaction and fullness of life's energy in a child or an adult. This adjustment in the idea of the functionality of the two brains gives encouragement to the idea that Human Nature will ultimately manage its own life. With less interference from civil and religious law, natural law and self-learning can, and will take over the responsibility for Human behavior. So let us explore longevity as a function of self-learning.

Less Stress as an Approach to Longevity

When the two brains are working together in support of the life center, they are the source of life's energy for the individual organism. There are two conditions that interfere with support of this cooperation of the two brains in the young child. The first happens often and is when a child is born and placed in an unsuitable environment where the necessary instinctual needs of freedom and attention are not available until the child enters school. The second condition that interferes with the life support given by the two brains working together is if the child enters school and the instincts are suppressed by the culture's rules, dogma, or laws. Both conditions provide stress to the organism. As a result, some of the children will rebel. Others will be able to find positive attention and freedom from interaction with others and overcome this environment challenge. What ever the quality of the aging experience, it tends to leave its mark on the aging animal. The more the needs are satisfying to the organism, the more it is living a full life of wellness. Less stress should sponsor less illness.

The quality of a life is determined by the coordinated effort of two dedicated systems—ENS and CNS—and the environment. The evaluation of the quality of life takes place in the ENS, which has a major roll of determining and recording what the quality should be, since it carries all the instructions of conception—its genetic inheritance. The ENS also has the power for providing energy to the entire organism, and the authority to regulate the CNS behavior when its attention strays away from its assignment. So we have self-control built into the organism with CNS furnishing and recording the activities of the environment—to protect the organism. We may be able to find these functional activities quite useful in our quest for understanding the aging process. We are suggesting here that wherever there exists reproductive growing bodies, they will contain some element of life and behavior that support Human Nature.

To see our Human Nature clearly, we need to be willing to accept Human Life, in principle, as just another form of life with its own functionality, as every other form of life—animal and vegetable—and of all species that operate with a different time schedule from that of the microbe to that of the giant

95

sequoia tree. These forms of life provide external structures, which are in time able to provide some selective use to each other, ultimately in the form of food, useful energy, or waste.

Taking this idea further, we can use a flowering stationery plant or shrub to compare two similar forms of life. The plant has two major systems working together—root, stem, and leaves with flower, fruit, and seed. The plant is immobile but it overcomes this factor by spreading many more seeds, some spread by wind, some spread by birds, and some spread by animals—including Humans.

Plants have their own means of protection; some by poison, some by prickly stems, some by beauty. Plants have roots to circulate moisture from the ground up through the tubes in the stems. Some carry liquids to keep the plants stems turgid, others carry nourishment and hormonal stimulation to the upper part of the plant to initiate leafing and flowering. The means of the liquid transport up the plant stems to the top of the plant is a simple use of the chemistry of water. There is no pressure pump to push it up against the pressure of the atmosphere. So nature uses water's attraction to itself and pulls it up through micro tubes to the leaves where it aspirates through the leaves into the air.

The flowers are a plant's version of the Human birth after being injected by a male sperm when needed. So plants have their own needed intelligence as do Humans, a set of instincts that are designed to establish all life and perpetuate that type of life according to its needs. We should now be able make a new connection with all life—with anything that grows.

There are many opportunities for dis-eases and traumas to enter any form of life development. In our attempt to understand the process of loss of effective use of the sensory brain, we will simplify the feeling by using only the name *Stress* for any variation from the balance of the ENS and the CNS becomes *Stressful* to the organism.

We have begun this exploration knowing that the environment in which most of us live (or have lived in our past) has been stressed by a culture, which tends to deny our animal nature, establishing an almost constant level of stress by denying our instincts and distrusting gut feelings.

In the 1970s, we discovered pure feelings using the Somatic Reflection Process (SRP) in stress therapy with college students. When the source of a trauma was found using feelings (ENS), we asked the student to think, using the(CNS), about the accuracy of the trauma he or she had found. There usually were two separate answers. The logic had recorded the details, and the gut feelings had recorded the impact of the experience on the individual. So all through life, the sensory brain could trigger the feelings of stress in the life center, (ENS).

Until we are willing and able to eliminate these stressful memories, we need to expect some affect on the energy available to the sensory brain. The digestive system may be expecting to maintain a balance of a full life, while the stress of the negative memories make it an impossible effort to balance the CNS and the ENS.

Experiencing Age, In Reverse

Let us concentrate on life in your past, and try to measure the satisfaction you feel in your stomach, as you start with the early childhood and work toward the present, reflecting somatically on how it felt to be you from moment to moment. This is certainly a form of reflection, but with the purpose of dealing

97

with issues that have interfered with your peace of mind as long as you can remember. That exercise (see the Somatic Reflection Process protocol in *What's Behind Your Belly Button?*) , when finished, will leave you stress free to begin a preparation to live, rather than a preparation for death that a person in stress may be concentrating upon (fearing). This exercise can begin whenever you can feel the need for freedom and acceptance. This reduction of stress leaves the body and mind more at ease, to project and enjoy a more positive self-image with others. Having *cleaned* out stressful experiences of the inner intelligence, we may now continue to age using our instincts to guide us in healthy life decisions.

It is the natural duty of the sensory brain to protect the body and the life processes in the human body. Stress that has transpired over long periods of time, weakens the gut feeling intelligence of the Enteric Nervous System from misuse. Such a possibility can be seen as a newborn is permitted to openly develop its instinctual skills until it begins to think for itself. Unfortunately after that period of time, adult judgment and logic is imposed and usually takes over, and the child is brought up to the sensory standards of the culture—of its environment—and feelings become unimportant. Confusion sets in, in the form of emotions like fear, guilt and hostility.

It would seem to us that where individuality losses any portion of its importance to any form of life—voluntary or imposed—we find a weakness in the quality of that individual life. Not until the latter part of the 20th Century was there a medical breakthrough to challenge and evaluate this idea. Unfortunately this standard of life quality idea has devastated many facets of most cultures concerning intelligence, learning, decision-making, Human need, stress, and disease. As we go back through our record of feeling memories, we will recognize the negative affects this idea has had on our Human Nature—both individually and collectively. And we find that we have been living with this poor standard of life quality without realizing Human Nature is weakening and dying. This recognition of our buried feelings is an important process of healing.

A Sound Solution

Think a moment about all of the infants, born without any visible experience, yet all displaying the same understanding of "where to go from here?". This understanding is not intelligence gained from its outside world, but it is the accumulation of intelligence passed along from others who have preceded it. It was noted and called the *collective unconscious* by Swiss Depth Psychiatrist Carl Jung. This intelligence turns out to be the ancient formula for life learned by all species as needed to perpetuate another useful generation of the same species. The next generation will add what little it learned that makes the life center more flexible and adaptable in the future. This process had a major roll to play in the beginning of all life on earth. Once we have accepted all animal life as having been gradually modified over eons of time by the experiences of generations of each new offspring with a new set of genes, we can begin to think in terms of modifying this intelligence for the common good. The Human intelligence that we would hope to modify through education and nurturing would be the ability to express openly the instinctual needs of Freedom and Acceptance. As we like to reiterate over and over, Human Beings are the only animal species—homo sapiens—that cannot openly use the brains with which they were born.

99

Unfortunately, any interference with the instincts at any time, in any way will run the risk of disturbing the intelligence of that life, and that life center.

There is one clear necessary change we must understand. As long as we try to control the Human instincts in our learning institutions and elsewhere, we will first, waste the necessary energy with which Humans have been given at birth. The consequence of the waste of energy will be to slow down the maturation of the sensory brain. If the sensory brain is not functioning well when it is required to help solve important problems—without the experience to do so—the solution will contain mostly guess work. Our Human thinking brain operates by way of prediction, comparing new experiences to and constructing its perception from what is already believed to be true due to past experiences. Without a mature intuition— thinking and feeling balanced and united—even groups trying to work together will only be capable of experiencing what has been going on in the sensory brain since about the 8th Century to the present.

Weakening
The Center of Life

Carefully observing a newborn child through its early experience of sensory growth, gives us an opportunity to see the instincts at work, seemingly without a conscious goal. We are well aware, however, that it is struggling with the energy that is generated by its own center of life, toward the perfection of its species—its genetic goal. As we follow the child's progress, we may reflect on our own life and realize that we rarely remember anything during the first one or two year's of life as we struggle with our own sensory development (although there is a feeling memory recorded in our gut feelings). Also, the child will most likely not remember those sensory-empty years. What the physical activity is about is the carrying out of the genetic plan by the DNA (the designer) and RNA (the builder) in order to finish the protection of the fetus in the outside world as soon as possible after birth. In spite of all the planning, effort, and energy expended in the process, we are trained to misunderstand the loss of need that is registered by the instincts as the loss of attention or the loss of self-control. In succeeding years, these early innocent happenings grow like weeds and become, when reminded (triggered), as a source of negative self-esteem throughout a lifetime. These accidents need to be corrected as soon as they are found, by reflecting somatically (feeling into the body) with our own feelings.

If we have lived a life focused on the outside world of things— those things into which we have provided a great amount of personal energy like something (a job or house or car) or someone we highly valued, then aging can feel like a loss of life. If we have lived a life focused on our Human Nature, we focus less on the details and more on the necessities of life. If we take this as a paradigm of our life—how we have learned to evaluate our personal life's experiences—we may find some of the causes for the ultimate loss of things that lead to the waste of energy, stress and even disease. The sad aspect of this theory of stressful aging and disease, is that we have shifted our attention away from the center of life—the instincts—and have tried to satisfy our needs from the external world. The results feel shameful to us (not accomplishable and thus like a failure as life weakens in old age or disease). If the instincts are suppressed and therefore unable to be consciously used and educated, we

101

will be forever observing the part of our life that we missed as a newborn. Remember, the instincts are here to stay as long as individual life exists.

A Life of Instinctual Awareness

Instinctual awareness has little creditability as long as the animal instincts in Humans are under pressures from the outside world, because the animal instincts are essential to the functional health and intelligence of Human life and can not be consciously used if suppressed. This statement does not mean that instincts are ever not available or un-useable. It does mean that the Human instincts are subject to control (may be suppressed) by outside pressure of civil law and are highly influenced by religious dogma. In modern cultures, they are generally allowed to be free only until the sensory brain of the newborn matures, enters the culture, and begins to think for his/herself. We have spent much space in this book describing the importance of the new born being free to use its instincts to develop the sensory brain—with a minimum of outside world interference. The reason for this lengthy discussion about the newborn is because it is the time that there is a clear display of the Human instincts and because that time of life sets the foundation for the health and satisfaction of the entire life processes.

The newborn infant is our purest living model of Human instincts that we have to observe. If we want to understand the essence of who we are as Human beings, it is the baby that we need to focus our attention upon and observe. In our observation, we might ask ourselves, if for the infant to grow up properly then do we need to change it by manipulating it into what we think it should be? Or can we concentrate upon nurturing the infant and assisting it to be what it already has the capacity and will to regulate itself to be? This is a big question, perhaps bigger than life itself. Much in politics, religion, education, and even medical and natural sciences throughout history, from era to era, has been an extension of the answer we have decided upon either one way or the other to this question.

Since we have never had a full understanding and definition of what our Human Nature truly is, we propose that even in eras that were more supportive of our inner nature, we have never had a culture that fully and consciously supported our Human instincts.

Presently, we have far too many people not supporting full Human intelligence (which includes instincts), therefore not helping us go forward as a Human species. However, we feel that it is both imperative for our species' survival and also that it is the right evolutionary time in Human history for us to explore once again this fundamental question of who we are instinctually. Modern technology has made it possible for Human beings to now be far more global community-minded than ever before. Thus, many people are beginning to embrace an inclusive view of the entire Human family, with common instinctual needs.

In order to answer the important question of whom we basically are inside, we must fully understand that society has never answered this question before with any depth or true accuracy from the point of view of life in the process of being lived, as a feeling experience. It has always defined our instincts by observing Humans from an external point of reference, from what behavior we see. We are saying that we cannot possibly understand whom we are inside through observation but instead must define our Human Nature and instincts through inner feeling reflection. We have suggested that we begin by looking at the "baby" to see what the infant is capable of and knows at birth, but our perception in this observation needs to be with the eye of understanding how the infant feels and what needs the infant indicates that they have.

Of course this type of observation of need has been done already by every parent who ever had an infant and also attempted by some scientists, such as developmental, child, and social psychologists. Yet, we have missed just what these instincts are other than the will to physical survival and have not make a substantial claim to our most Human instincts, that which drives us throughout life, other than the biological ones. For this reason, we began our discussion in this book by redefining what these unclaimed Human instincts are, or at least what we have found them to be with the many people we have somatically reflected on gut feelings with in counseling sessions and who have reported awareness of early feeling memory.

Now that we have defined these Human instincts (freedom/self-control and acceptance/attention), then we shall look to see how we might best honor them and begin to nurture Humans as they age to be all that they can be and to live a full and long life. Of course, aging begins the second we are born (and some would argue from the moment of conception), so our Human story of instinctual aging begins there!

Achieving Longevity Through Instinctual Awareness

Your gut instincts are directly connected to your inner needs to be accepted (attention) and feel in control of your responses, and research now shows that developing both of these can lead to two of the most important skills for achieving longevity and enjoying the experience of aging.

Researchers have recently been interested in what factors allow centenarians to reach age 100 and beyond. While biological contributors relating to diet and genetics are certainly important and need further research, the newest emphasis is on epidemiological relationships between personality, physical health, and Human longevity. A study with 243 centenarians (average age was actually 97.5 years old and a majority were female) by researchers at Albert Einstein College of Medicine and Ferkauf Graduate School of Psychology of Yeshiva University (and a part of the research of Nir Barzilai, M.D., the Ingeborg and Ira Leon Rennert Chair of Aging Research) developed the Personality Outlook Profile Scale (POPS, we can only assume that there is no pun intended) to help determine what genetic personality traits might be significant for longevity. It shows that centenarians expressed their emotions openly rather than bottling them up. This was not actually what the researchers expected to find and they were a bit surprised that the centenarians did not survive longer than other people simply by "orneriness" but rather it was by being quite social. Centenarians tended to also have a large social network and to consider positive attitudes and laughing important in their lives. So they concluded that being outgoing and extraverted is an important personality trait in longevity. While changing one's typology from introvert to extrovert is not necessary or even truly possible, this study certainly indicates that whether you are extravert or introvert, learning to develop your instinctual awareness in order to unite body and mind and fulfill your need for acceptance (attention from others) is important. For those of you interested in this study it is called "Positive attitude towards life and emotional expression as personality phenotypes for centenarians."

Other longevity studies have also shown that personality does have an affect upon aging and that a more extraverted personality is helpful for increasing longevity. If you break down why and what this means, you see that it is because extraverts tend to go after what they need in the world around them more than introverts (introverts gather their energy primarily from the inner world of ideas), particularly when it comes to human relations and attention from others.

While social connection and human relations are found to be both vital to longevity, there are other longevity factors including inherited factors like genetics, diet, educational level, lifestyle, and also the characteristics of the community environment that elders live in. How possible it is for elders to achieve social connectedness in their environments has been found to be significant to achieving longevity. Although opportunity for sociability does also need to be available, the extravert is more likely to reach out and forge new friendships in elder years and to satisfy their needs for acceptance and attention, an important instinctive need.

Furthermore, feeling in control is another characteristic state that researchers now attributes to longevity. An extensive longevity study with over 6000 people by Nicolas Turiano and Benjamin Chapman of the University of Rochester Medical

Center, Frank Infurna of the German Institute for Economic Research, and Stefan Agrigoroaei of Brandeis in 2014 (see *Journal of Health Psychology,* Vol 33(8)) points to the fact that people who feel a high sense of being in control have less risk of mortality. Here we are talking about the feeling that one can achieve goals despite hardships. The study found that feeling in control is even more important than the person's level of education (which also has significant positive affects upon longevity).

So one can see why preparing early in life for our elder years by learning to follow your gut instincts to fulfill your inner needs is so important. Both of the instinctual needs—acceptance and control—are referred to as important in research conclusions on desirable personality traits for longevity. We will take this up further in unit five on Instinctual Awareness and the Medical Profession when we talk about personalized medicine.

We need models of how to live long, satisfying lives using our instincts and accepting our inner nature. There is an increase in life expectancy worldwide. A marker for longevity in a person is how long the parents of that person live. So, if you have a parent that lives to 100, then you as the off spring have an increased chance to do so yourself, and even beyond. It is not clear by scientists why this is so other than possible genetics, but that has not been conclusive in research. We suggest that there is a learning process that goes on and is passed down to the younger generation—the process of learning how to cope with aging using ones instincts successfully. We could call this the *trial and learning* process of aging. Once we have a model to follow and we have some experience to learn from our elders that come before us, we have a chance of coping more successfully and lengthening our longevity and quality of life in old age.

We need a model of how to cope in old age successfully, of how to reach out to others and forge relationships despite the lack of mobility, how to interact and accept caring from caregivers and medical care, how to make new friends within our limited environment, how to keep moving, and perhaps most of all, how not to degrade our feeling of self-acceptance in the face of having both less in the world around us and an aging body.

It is the model of the *trial and learn* process of instinctual aging that helps a person to experience heightened longevity. And perhaps it is possible that an elder who lives closely aligned with his or her instincts but is not genetically related to you, may also pass on to you the gift of longevity by being a model that you follow. If this is true, then the greatest gift from an elderly to another person is the gift of *trial and learn* and modeling to us successful aging. When an elder is in touch with their instincts and lives each day reaching out with gratitude to satisfy their inner needs, we all learn an important lesson. It is important to remember to thank such elders for being important models and showing us the way. We feel it is quite possible that association with elders that are successful in providing us a model of aging with instincts would be beneficial to any younger person's health and longevity.

Part 3

Gut Feelings and Intuitional Intelligence in Applied Modern Psychology

On Emotions, Developing Intuition, Body Awareness, Happiness, Memory, Fear of Death and Dying, Decision-Making, Inner Human Needs, Social Bonds and Marriage, Relationships, & the Therapeutic Process

Increasing Your Intuitive Intelligence By Learning the Difference Between Emotional Feelings & Gut Feelings

This is an important essay in psychological literature as it gives the steps necessary for our Human species to increase our *Intuitive Intelligence*. It explores Daniel Goleman's theory of Emotional Intelligence and suggests that we need to go even further in our consciousness through gut feeling awareness to make another step toward our evolution of intelligence.

Since the publication of our first book on the intelligence of gut feeling responses, we have been combing the internet daily (with the help of Google Alerts) to read what people are saying on the subject of gut intelligence. Perhaps the one thing that we are most pleased about finding in our search is that people are recognizing that gut instincts and feelings are important in their lives—that they are important to at least listen to—although people are continually recognizing and expressing some concern that they do not fully understand them. We'd like to explore this question of what these gut feelings are and how they relate to intuition. We believe that the answer lies in a deeper understanding of the difference in emotional feelings and gut feelings.

Psychologist and Science Journalist Daniel Goleman was the first to popularize the understanding in psychology that our feelings and thinking are different and that it is important to learn the difference, to increase *Emotional Intelligence*. He linked emotional intelligence to success and healthy living. Up until Goleman's work, we had the theories of Personality Type of Carl Jung that pointed to the difference in Thinking (logic) and Feeling (value) as functions, and, working off that, the Myers Briggs Type Indicator (MBTI). Although quite valuable, Jung's theories did not make a clear distinction showing that feelings are in the body (and originating from the gut) and logic in the head brain.

After a number of years of an active humanistic movement, people slowly began learning in the 70s and 80s the difference in their body and head responses, feeling and thinking. But now, it seems we may be finally understanding that we need to go a little further with our Emotional Intelligence and learn the difference in the emotions and in the gut feelings. Remember, as we have previously said in this book, that when we speak of our gut feelings, we are talking about the emptiness/fullness feeling in the gut that is related to our inner needs and to a balance of being in control of our responses to life (freedom) and of the need for acceptance (attention). We have pointed out that this is different from the emptiness that is due to the lack of food intake, although we often mistake it for the emptiness of hunger and thus find ourselves over-eating. Until we reflect upon our gut feelings of emptiness and fullness and reassess our past experiences through somatic reflection on the gut region of our bodies, we will be clouded with old inaccurate

112

patterns of memories in our thinking and our intuition just will be buried in our consciousness and unclear as well.

Irrational feelings are our emotions, not the feelings in our guts, although unfortunately often confused. Let us explain briefly the difference between emotions and gut feelings, because we think this is a key to the increase of our intuitive intelligence and also to the question of how we know that our gut feelings are reliable:

1. Emotions are generally felt above the gut, above the Hara, and are a combination of feeling from the gut and thinking from the head, i.e. fear, a combination of emptiness in gut feeling combined with a projection from the head as to a specified threat.

2. Gut feelings, felt in the Hara, have no thinking component like emotions do; gut feelings are pure feeling of emptiness or fullness and they are the source of all feeling in emotions.

3. Gut feelings are pure feeling and relate to the state of the Human organism.

4. Gut feelings are your truth, so to speak, related to how well your needs for acceptance and for feeling in control of your own responses to life/freedom is being met, and they are in that way always a reliable response about your instinctual needs as a Human Being.

It can take quite a bit of reflection on our gut feelings to begin to understand the difference in emotions and gut feelings, to see this in your own experience, particularly if you are not use to exploring feelings on this level and distinguishing the difference in emotions and gut feelings. But just like it is so important to understand the difference in thinking and feeling to increase our Emotional Intelligence, it is important to take the time to understand the difference in emotional feelings and

113

gut feelings to further increase our intelligence and facility of intuition that we like to call *Intuitional Intelligence*. We may have increased our *Emotional Intelligence* by understanding the difference in our thinking and feelings or emotions, but let's go further and begin to develop our Intuitive Intelligence by understanding and reflecting upon the difference in our emotional feelings and gut feelings.

Simply said, we need to explore our gut instincts, not just use them with some vague idea of what they are. One really has to "Know Thyself" and take the effort to do that inner work to use their gut feelings successfully in decision-making. We have found in our counseling and research that there is much more to our gut instincts than just "pattern recognition brain impressions" as some have suggested, although these patterns are certainly a result of our gut intelligence combined with our thinking—and the accuracy of our thinking depends upon whether we use our gut feelings as a premise of our thinking or leave out the impact of experience upon us and marginalize our human needs as unimportant to consider in problem-solving. This all affects the accuracy and haze in these mental patterns and our ability to have and increase Intuitive Intelligence. If we use our thinking as a premise for our logic without grounding it in our gut feelings (the emptiness and fullness in our guts), we run the risk of following a system of thought coming from an external source that may not take our human needs in consideration nor have any relevance to our life experience.

You may be asking at this point, is intuition and gut feeling instincts the same. While you must become aware of your gut feelings in order to develop your intuition, they are not the same. Gut feeling instinct is a response center in the Hara that we are born with (the emptiness and fullness feeling that

114

responds to how well our needs of acceptance and freedom are being met from moment-to-moment) and we can become more and more adapt at listening to it. Once we begin listening to our gut instinctual responses, our body and mind begin to work in unison and we have intuitive thoughts (possibilities that arise in our awareness). Intuition is then developed. This is true mind (gut, head and some would say even heart all working together without blocks or oppositions from external forces like other people's thoughts). So, gut instinctual feelings are something we are born with and intuition is something we develop. We all have the potential for developing intuitive intelligence, but must work from the bottom up, from Hara to Head, to experience this intelligence. This is why taking the time to reflect somatically on your gut feelings is so important if you would like to increase your Intuitional Intelligence.

Have you ever felt like you were out on a limb trying to follow someone else's ideas of what you should be doing—even someone you carry in your memory and haven't seen for a long time? We have to reflect on our gut feelings to separate out the thinking in our heads that comes from someone else's view of us, perhaps a view we picked up so long ago that we have forgotten when we first thought it or where it really came from. Successful people stop when they have emotional feelings like fear and begin to reflect and listen to their own deeper gut feelings and needs and take those into consideration in their goal setting and actions. When your thinking and gut feelings in your body are united, you feel confident and like you are standing on solid ground. This is also a condition that reduces stress and brings on good health, as well as intuitive and creative thinking, or Intuitional Intelligence.

It takes inner work to truly recognize our gut feelings, to tell the difference in gut feelings from emotional feelings, and to understand what about you and your instinctive needs that your gut feelings are expressing, thus to understand the impact of experience upon you and lay the foundation for an increase in your Intuitive Intelligence. We have found that people find that their intuition and healthy decision-making increases exponentially with somatic reflection on the awareness of one's gut feelings of emptiness and fullness. A reflection into your past through gut feeling awareness to reassess the meaning of your experiences and update your "thinking patterns", conscious and unconscious, is a healing and healthy experience that takes you into the next level of understanding your *feeling body* and will flood your awareness with higher Intuitive Intelligence.

The Development of Body Awareness and Instincts in Modern Psychology

Psychology is a relatively new science and its root beginnings was centered around experimental psychology, with Wilhelm Wundt founding the first exclusive psychology laboratory in 1879. While psychology had already begun to make an imprint upon the general population, it was not until the late 1960s and early 1970s with the flourishing of Humanistic and Somatic Psychology that it began to give us the vocabulary to talk about our inner world and to influence how we communicate what we feel inside with each other in every day life. We feel that it is important to include in this book a short synopsis of some of these other early and modern psychological theorists and practitioners who explored the wisdom of the body/instincts and found as we have that the Human psyche is self-regulatory.

*U*ntil quite recently, the awareness of the body and human instincts has not had an important place in modern psychology. Here is a short history of some of those in the field of psychology who first focused on mind-body unity (it is a brief and certainly does not include all who are so important in this field). They point the way toward the realization that the answer to who we are and the intelligence of our Human Nature is in the awareness of feelings in the body, with the inner wisdom to be self-regulatory.

While Carl Jung warned against neglecting the awareness of instincts and viewed the act of dissilience with the unconscious as being synonymous with the loss of instinct, he was vague in his *Collective Works* on the relationship of instincts and the body and particularly on the importance of the awareness of feeling in the body. The awareness of the relationship of the mind and body has more recently become a focus of study in psychology. This new focus in modern psychology views the relationship of the body and mind as functioning as a unit rather than as separate. It can be traced back to the establishment of Somatic Psychology by Wilhelm Reich. Techniques developed by Reich

117

encourage emotional release through exercises that emphasis awareness of the body.

Many modern psychologists agree that we must turn to the awareness of our bodies to experience the inner self or essence of our being. Clinical psychologist David Abram in *The Spell of the Sensuous* defines the self as our inner most essence that is experienced within the body rather than as a transcendental and disembodied experience. He views the idea of experiencing self or mind as an "immaterial phantom ultimately independent of the body" (p. 45) to be an illusion and unfounded in actual sensory perception. Gestalt therapists Fritz Perls, Paul Goodman, and Ralph Hefferline also disagree with the traditional meaning of the mind as "a disembodied something, which transcends organic functioning" (see *Gestalt Therapy: Excitement and Growth in the Human Personality*, page 17). In their view the mind and body are one, and mind can only function within the body. Abram's theories mirror this view with the idea that without the living body, there is no possibility of contact with others or with oneself in the reflection process. He points out that there is no way for us to be conscious of ourselves or of others without a living body.

The importance of turning to the awareness of the body to assess the impact of life experience upon the individual is addressed by modern day Jungians such as John Conger in his work *Jung & Reich: The Body As Shadow*. He recognizes the body as the container for the record of our rejected side, the shadow, "revealing what we dare not speak, expressing our current and past fears" (p.108). According to Conger, there is no way to have access to the deep interior of the unconscious without becoming aware of the body.

Jungian analyst Marion Woodman in *Addiction to Perfection* suggests that it is vital that we keep in touch with the wisdom of nature and the wisdom of our own instincts for the constant flow of energy toward health and well being of the psyche. "The ego can only be strong enough if it is supported by the wisdom of the body whose messages are directly in touch with the instincts (p. 16)." Woodman emphasizes the importance of body awareness work to awaken and release emotions often trapped in the body. And in her later book *Coming Home to Myself,* she emphasizes the importance of listening to the signals that the body gives us "as a reservoir of cellular memory, wisdom, and guidance" (p. 40). She asserts that attending to the signals of one's body, deepens awareness of the unconscious and leads one toward an awareness of wholeness of the psyche.

Identifying our instincts as signals of organismic needs may seem challenging for us. We often have a difficult time becoming aware of our feelings or felt sense. We may get our feeling and thinking functions confused, which makes it difficult to separate and identify them in our awareness. In *The Shaman's Doorway*, clinical psychologist Stephen Larson supports the idea that there is a difference between the feeling experience and the assigned meaning or interpretation that we give an experience. Larson also saw that we often get the two confused.

Philosopher and psychotherapist Eugene T. Gendlin warns in his book *Experiencing and the Creation of Meaning* that we often confuse the experiencing moment of a felt experience with the meaning we have assigned it. Larson further supports Gendlin's idea that the felt experience is an "a-priori, instinctive impulse" that occurs in a pre-conceptual, the

119

moment before all thought or assigned meaning. He assigns the felt experiencing as having a primary meaning or meaning that precedes description with words. When we explain the felt experience with a verbal description, we are experiencing a secondary meaning that follows the initial instinctive impulse. This secondary meaning is a feeling-thought combination derived from the original feeling.

According to Larson, this differentiation between felt experience and interpretation is often lost in our awareness of the experience. This points to the idea that we could have layers of feelings in our psyche with feeling-interpretation combinations on the surface layer, and the deepest layer consisting of pure feeling or instinctual feelings. The difficulty in the differentiation between felt experience and interpretation could explain why we are often not aware of the difference between these layers, between emotion and gut feeling.

In *Gestalt Therapy Verbatim*, psychotherapist Fritz Perls speaks to the difficulty of being aware of instinctual, organismic needs as a reliable point of reference. External thoughts we have learned to follow often replace awareness of the instinctual organismic needs. He views "the organism as a system that is in balance" (p. 16), and he strives to have people experience themselves as self-regulatory rather than externally regulated. Perls speaks of the pathology of self-manipulation interfering with the self-control of the organism. He finds that the organism typically follows an external thought pattern rather than its own wisdom. Perls noted that the word self-manipulating is interesting because we may see an immediate problem with the idea of manipulating others (or being manipulated by others) without any idea that we are manipulating ourselves with external thought patterns. He demonstrates with this idea that we are

120

often unaware that we are living our lives from an external point of view and denying our own inner wisdom.

Modern neuroscientists generally agree with the idea that our thinking brain has little consciousness of ourselves without the awareness of the body. David Eagleman, director of a neuroscience research laboratory at Baylor College of Medicine in the Texas Medical Center, views the importance of the enteric nervous system as not being regulated by our mental ideas nor even accessed completely through our thinking brain, and that the conscious "you" has little control over the greater physical part of "oneself". He suggests that you cannot really "know thyself" simply through thinking who you are, as you will be void of knowledge of much of yourself.

"Knowing yourself now requires a change of definition of "to know". Knowing yourself now requires the understanding that the conscious you occupies only a small room in the mansion of the brain, and that is has little control over the reality constructed for you. The invocation to know thyself needs to be considered in new ways." — David Eagleman in *Incognito: The Secret Lives of the Brain*

Conclusions on the Affects on Longevity of Increased Feeling Awareness and Communication

Until the emergence of the psychologists that we have traced in this discussion, Western modern humanity had little language to communicate inner feelings and certainly had little body feeling conscious awareness. Some Eastern cultures have had language to describe feelings and feeling experiences far longer than Western cultures. There are still today some words in Japanese, for instance, that can not be translated into English because English does not have the vocabulary to express certain Human feeling experiences.

Today, we even have popular TV talk shows that demonstrate to us how to talk to each other about our inner feelings, something that was just not possible in the 50s before psychology gave us the vocabulary to do so in the 60s and 70s. It is our opinion that the input of psychological awareness of body-mind unity along with the contribution of psychological language of our feelings has had a great affect upon Humanity's ability to communicate using our instincts and thus live longer, healthier lives. We even go so far as to conjecture that our overall improved ability to communicate our feelings is one reason that general longevity has increased in the recent decades, despite the rise of stress in modern technological life.

Exploring Gut Feelings
and Happiness

Much of modern psychology is centered around finding happiness or Happiness Psychology. This next short discussion explores the importance of being conscious of gut feelings in order to attain fulfillment in life that leads to genuine happiness.

It is true that we cannot always change the world outside of us to our liking, so we are challenged to look inside for the answers to living a more fulfilled life and in hopes of finding some sense of clarity on what to do in problem-solving of unresolved issues.

It does not help to keep focusing on the details in the present unresolved issue, but a new perspective may be found by focusing on the feelings within you and tracing them back in time to their origin. In counseling people who find themselves constantly in conflict with a spouse or loved one, for instance, we have often used the metaphor that "you can't use one empty bucket to fill another empty bucket, unless you go take it to the well first and get some fresh water." Meaning, you may just keep reinforcing negative feelings in each other if you are both feeling empty. So, before you decide that your life situation is hopelessly doomed to disparity and that there is no resolution or positive steps to resolve a present issue in your life (or love relationship), it is important to continue (or start whichever it may be) the inner work of healing yourself through somatically reflecting on gut feelings and uniting your head and gut. It is often hard to accept, but the real conflict and source of unhappiness is inside oneself. We have both the ability and need to resolve these inner issues relating to our own past experiences so we can move forward with assuredness and success and attain happiness.

Our effect upon the world around us, and certainly including those things that seem to cause us the most difficulty, is minimized by our own sense of uncertainly about ourselves and by our self-doubts, by those things in our past that are still unresolved within us and that are still being triggered in our feelings and confusing our perspective of the now, and by our feelings of emptiness and aloneness. So let's start there in our exploration to find wellness.

It amazes most people how much they are still carrying around feelings from unresolved issues in their past and responding from feelings related to those unresolved experiences and are, thus, in some ways still in the "sandbox" at around age 4 to 6, even prior to going to school. This is hard to understand until you begin feeling into the issue you are most concerned about and reflecting on earlier times you felt this way. Then you find that this has been an issue in your feelings for many years and started perhaps very early in your life. Our original feeling experience is like a little snow ball beginning to roll down a giant hill, it picked up more and more snow as it went speeding down the hill, until it became a huge ball resting at the bottom. Finding the source so we can clear up our unresolved feelings takes some deep somatic reflection, but generally feels freeing and relieving and gives us clarity, hope, and leads us toward a life of true happiness.

Exploring Gut feelings About the Fear of Death and Dying

This essay addresses the question of why we fear death and gives some suggestions of what to do to deal with one's fears.

Why do we fear death some days more than others? Have you ever ask yourself that question? We all know that there are some days or times in our lives that we buzz along without a thought of death, as we are too busy living and engaged in the now to concern ourselves with such thoughts. These can be our most healthy and productive moments. But then something happens to wake us up to the stark awareness that we are mortal. And this awareness does not have to come through a crisis in our lives, although it certainly may, but through what appears to be a threat of a meaningful loss of life quality and a feeling of helplessness to adequately cope with the threat. You may have had a minor tooth ache/cavity that reminded you of death, suddenly becoming acutely aware of how easy it would be to slip downhill in health without proper heath care. Almost any slight ailment can remind us of death and question our preparedness for this journey. Like any journey, if we are prepared, we feel less anxious about it. When one fears death, then it is important to take the effort to be prepared for it.

Gut feeling awareness may be our best guide for understanding our authentic selves, improving our self awareness and increasing our intuition, and also for preparing us for meeting our own death and to lessen the fear of death. Obviously, how

125

calm we feel inside and how at peace we are with ourselves has an effect upon how we feel about our own death. We might say, then, that our best insurance for the future is to insure the "now" and resolve issues from our past so they are not crippling us with fear or blocking us from feeling alive and energized in the now. Once we feel good about ourselves in our past, we will not fear the future, and will feel perfectly in tune with our lives in our Now.

So if we want to stop fearing death, then we must start living fully in the Now and get out of the past. We are not saying to just "get over it" because we know that no one can really do that until they have come to some resolutions about their past first. But we are saying that the goal is to resolve the past in order to get actively engaged in the present moment, the Now. A quick way to get into the Now, although not lasting in itself, may be to do some activity that turns on our senses, so that we are getting fresh data input from the world around us. Activities like swimming, brisk walking, biking, and other sports, gardening, certainly art, even a leisurely walk in a new direction can give us a sense of Now-ness. And if we are very empty inside, it is advised to do something of this sort to turn your senses on before and after your meditations and somatic reflections on gut feelings. To experience more of the Now in life, you are looking to increase your perception, and that is a matter of both increasing your sensing function through activity and your intuition function through somatic reflection.

The very act of sharing how you feel can diminish fear, even of death, to a manageable amount. Understanding that the fear has to do with more than just the environment or situation at hand, but about how you feel in your life at the present time in general, is an important clue to know how to both reflect on

126

the feeling and share it. If you have been feeling lately a little out of control in your life in general, try to share that with a person close to you. It may have far more to do with how you are feeling about the present situation than you would think. Sharing your feelings will calm you and probably the listener too!

If you have no one to share these feelings with, then try writing it down. Journaling your feelings, either privately or in social networking if you feel comfortable with that, can be a big comfort.

We often found in counseling that people would find as they somatically reflected on their fear and then became closer to the source of their gut feelings, that they were experiencing the initial fear as a trigger of a time in their past that they perceived losses to have occurred. Once the past period with accompanying feelings of loss were brought to light and shared, people felt much better about the present and the fear was released. So we always suggest people use the Somatic Reflection Process to unravel the fear and become more self aware.

It is important to understand the anatomy of what your feeling of fear really is. Rather than indicating an outside danger over which we have no control, fear is often a necessary signal that indicates there is some emptiness inside of us. Somatically reflecting on the gut feeling of emptiness, exploring these feelings, and sharing them with a person that you trust can help you deal with even a gripping fear and unit your body-mind connection so you can function successfully.

Using the Gut Brain for Decision-Making in Intimate Relationships

In this chapter, we apply the image of the two-brain Human intelligence system to the popular subject of love relationships and using our gut feelings to make healthy life-decisions about relationships.

W e have found that the healthiest decisions people make when it comes to love relationships, are made from a place of self-awareness and the ability to communicate one's own needs. Our gut feelings are connected to a wealth of information, both conscious and unconscious, about our feeling memories and inner needs. If we have had difficult relationships earlier in our lives (either difficult romantic or family-personal relationships), then there is all the more reason to reflect upon our gut feelings to clear unresolved past issues and to avoid carrying them into a new relationship. You may be surprised how much your gut is holding, waiting for you to attend to your needs and use this inner knowledge to make healthy decisions.

Many people have written us and asked, "Can you trust your gut in love and marriage decisions?" Recent research (2013) at Florida State University lead by Social Psychologist Dr. James K. McNulty on what they are calling "gut feelings" of newlyweds and marriage success, has given cause to become interested in understanding gut feelings in relation to predicting

128

success in marriage. While the study was small—sample was only 135 heterosexual couples, it was significant in that it found that newlyweds know on a subconscious level (implicit memory) whether their marriage will be happy.

McNulty's study demonstrates something we have also found in counseling people who are in the throws of making life decisions in both personal relationships and career, which is that our gut feeling does not change just because we want it to or our head says it should. We are however, talking about true gut somatic feelings, not just implicit associations. But there is certainly a correlation between the two.

The findings in McNulty's study make sense particularly if you understand that your gut feelings of emptiness and fullness register how well your two instinctive needs of feeling accepted and also in control of your own responses (freedom) are being met from moment-to-moment. We found that if these two needs, acceptance and control, are in balance in relation to the impact on us of time spent with someone, people feel full in their gut feelings, cared for and loved for who they truly are.

We all know the emptiness and aloneness we feel in our guts when we do not feel free to be ourselves with someone and/or when there is a lack of attention (acceptance) in relation to the other person. We can rationalize in our heads that our needs are met by a relationship, but our gut feelings of emptiness or fullness are a true indication of how well our inner needs are being met and how close we truly feel to the other person.

Our gut is its own intelligence and is connected to the needs of our inner world or organism rather than to pleasing social demands or making money or any other goal that relates to our outer world and simply our thinking process without the input of our feeling memory. So, if your gut says that a relationship is

129

not quite right for you, it is important to listen to your feelings and take the time to understand what it is indicating about you. This certainly does not necessarily mean that if you have an empty feeling about a relationship that the relationship does not have the potential to work out, but it does indicate a need for self-reflection on gut feelings and communication with the other person—if it is to be a successful relationship.

A Word About the Relationship Between the Heart and Gut

Throughout history, the heart has been given all the credit for Human love and compassion, with the gut unrelated to this feeling. But if you look at it a little closer within yourself with some somatic reflection on your own gut feelings, you will come to see that your gut holds your feeling memory, and is the origin of your love for self and also for others. It is in the gut that you must start to be conscious of your self and accept (love) yourself before you can accept (love) anyone else. And it is in the gut center that people often have told us that they first felt a feeling of connection to others.

The gut response cannot be influenced to change just because your head says so (or because some one external to you says so). The gut response holds the meaning of the impact of all experience upon you and this memory is always there in your gut awaiting you to become conscious of it, access it, and explore it through somatic reflection (feeling into the gut, not just thinking back in time). Our gut feels full of positive energy if we feel accepted for who we are naturally, in control of our own responses to life and cared for by others. We all need to feel loved for who we truly are. If we do not have these two needs met, we know it in our guts, even if our heads are saying otherwise.

It is through the reflection on this gut feeling of empty-full, that we can trace back the impact of our life throughout time and reassess our thinking to unite our body and mind for wellness. Once we have achieved this unity through gut awareness, we feel a deep acceptance (love) for our own being as a part of and connected to the greater Humanity. And at this point of gut awareness, and only then, can our hearts open up to feel compassion and love for others.

Are Gut Feelings Reliable About Love Relationships

Perhaps the single one thing that we have been asked concerning gut feelings is: *"Is my gut feeling correct that my relationship is lacking something?"*

Our gut feelings hold the knowledge and feeling memory of the impact of our past experiences upon us. So we can listen to how we are feeling in regards to a present relationship and our gut will remember times in the past when we were experiencing something similar to what is being "triggered" in our feelings. We could be having a triggered memory from a time in which we were being ignored, the other person was unavailable, etc.. Or perhaps it could even be a triggered memory from early childhood—in a relationship of a different kind like a parent who is too tired from work to give us attention or often absent. We need to reflect back in time and center on that feeling in our guts (the emptiness) and see where it takes us—find its origin. Then as we look around inwardly while we are in that feeling memory, we will learn a lot about ourselves and our needs as a person.

Our gut may be holding a message for us that may be very important in making a current decision or it may be telling us that we still have something inside from our past that needs to be resolved within for the current relationship to work. Our gut may be both telling us that we are not getting what we need out of the current relationship and it may also be telling us that we need to explore inwardly and clear ourselves of past unresolved issues to help be consciously present enough ourselves to make this current relationship work.

We need to remember that for others to know us, we have to be willing to show them who we are and often we hide in our insecurities from others the best part of ourselves. Our gut feelings are often reminding us to come out of hiding so our relationship has a chance to grow.

A little time reflecting on your gut feelings and inner self now can save you much suffering in the future and help you avoid a relationship crisis. So be sure before you walk down that aisle to spend some somatic reflection time on your gut feelings! If you are already in a relationship and have an uneasy gut feeling about your relationship, then accessing your gut feeling intelligence may help you resolve issues from your past that are being triggered in and blocking your perception from being strictly related to the person with whom you are presently in a relationship. Exploring gut intelligence may well strengthen your present relationship through better communication and will undoubtedly lead you to more healthy personal decision-making that allows you to take your inner needs into account with a united body-mind, gut-head intelligence.

Reflecting on Gut Feelings to Deal with Sadness and Loss of Love Relationships

If we experience an emotion like sadness, we can be sure that our thinking brain (CSN) and our gut brain (ENS) are at odds with each other and not communicating completely, although they are certainly trying to do so. We need to separate them further so we can identify what each is saying to us, and that will allow us to bring in some fresh information about ourselves that will set the course of a natural unity of body-mind. In simpler terms, we have to center on how we are feeling emotionally and allow ourselves to look at both the thinking part of this emotion and the purely gut feeling part, then trace the source of those emotions and gut feelings in our understanding of the impact of our past experiences.

Generally we have found in using the Somatic Reflection Process with people who were experiencing sadness and relationship loss, that the sadness was related to a past experience in which they assumed some guilt for the loss, blaming themselves. The sadness that we encountered in the hundreds of people we counseled was generally found in somatic reflection to be largely related to a feeling of guilt.

The feeling of guilt is the same feeling of emptiness whether a person has taken on the thinking judgment that they did or did not do something particular that caused or contributed to their loss or whether they took on the judgment that they were too small and inadequate, unprepared, ill-informed, not-good enough or unaware to act in a manner that would have avoided the loss. In either of these judgments, the resulting feeling emotion is guilt.

133

Often, when we ask people for the first time if they can see a relationship to their feeling of sadness to the feeling of guilt, they think we mean something they have done wrong, for which they will say "no". But once they examine their feelings, they see their sadness has a thinking component of how they think they were "not powerful enough or good enough" and this realization of a "less than" feeling or guilt opens a door of perception up. It is much easier to deal with one's feeling of guilt from the past and find the source of the judgments that we have put upon ourselves (generally back in early childhood where we originally accepted judgments from authorities or others who did not understand how we felt inside) than it is to deal with a profound feeling of sadness and loss for which we have no control or we think simply relates to some event in recent times or adulthood.

Generally, our adult romantic losses trigger feelings unresolved from earlier life and are even set up to happen because we have not cleared our understanding of ourselves in this earlier event. It does take quite a bit of reflecting on the impact of life upon you—your gut feelings—to reassess your past and understand that you are perfectly Human, that you care in your instinctual feelings, and that you always have been caring. But until we do find our caring and loving nature inside, we will not feel we deserve love and happiness, and that is our biggest loss.

Gut Feelings As the Key to Further Development of Memory Theories in Psychology

> The following discusses some of the latest research and memory theories in psychology concerning adults remembering childhood experiences. From our experience using the Somatic Reflection Process with adults to access past feeling memories of the impact of experiences going back into early childhood, we suggest that the gut feeling response is the key to childhood memory recovery.

W e are educators and school counselors, not neurologists, and although we could certainly speculate, we would not presume to say that we know why in a biological sense that reflecting on gut feelings is key to personal memory. However, from our extensive counseling experiences with the Somatic Reflection Process on gut feelings, we have observed that there is a strong psychological relationship between gut feelings and memory. It is as though reflecting on how one has felt in their gut in the past, begins to awaken feeling memory in the majority of people and this triggers even memory of external events or at least what the person assumed was true at the time of the event. We therefore, feel from this experience that memory theorists and researchers in the field are amiss if they do not explore the functional relationship of gut feelings to memory.

Many people say that they cannot remember their childhood experiences prior to age 7 and memory studies by psychologists

135

in the field of childhood development will tell you that this is normal. Dr. Patricia Bauer, Professor of Psychology and Senior Associate Dean of Research at Emory University in Atlanta, GA, has been researching the development of memory in children since the 80s. She has found that children begin to have a significant increase in the rate of forgetting memories of their past life events after the age of 7, or the onset of what was termed by Sigmund Freud as Childhood Amnesia.

For a long time, it was thought that the reason many adults could not remember events from their early childhood was because young children just did not have memory ability. But that has since been explored in research and Bauer concludes children do have memory ability but that memories from earlier than age 7 have an accelerated rate for being forgotten once the child is past age 7 than the memories formed after that age. Why the onset of this forgetting process is at age 7 is still in question and has lead to further important memory studies of children.

What is important here to us is that the memory research now being conducted on children concludes that recovering childhood memories is important to the development of personal identity and adult decision-making. This is a welcome validation of our work developing and using the Somatic Reflection Process on gut feelings to recover memory, with the affect of uniting body and mind in consciousness. The importance of recovering childhood memories is an understanding that we as career counselors have used in our clinical studies with people since the 70s, as we found that the seeds of who we are and who we become begin in early childhood. If we can become conscious of those beginnings, then we have valuable self-awareness information upon which to base healthy and successful life decisions as adults.

In our counseling work, we found something very shocking to many people who had no prior or very little childhood memories. When we asked people to center their awareness on their gut feelings to guide them and slowly to go back in time and remember when they felt a particular feeling in their gut before, they would be able nearly 100% of the time to access early childhood memories previously un-recalled. And those people who had previously been able to recall childhood memories were able to continue to recall additional memories using this gut feeling reflection process.

Gut Feelings as the Key to Feeling String Theory

We discovered that the key to recovering childhood memories was to have people focus on their inner gut feelings and impact of experience rather than the details of their lives. We would ask them to come in their awareness to a place in their past when they had the same feeling they were centering on in the present (usually starting with a reoccurring feeling connected to an unresolved issue in the present time of their life) and then they would allow the details of the experience in the past to come to their own minds. Each time a feeling memory would come up in their consciousness, they were asked to focus on the feeling and continue to go back further in time. It was as if their present feeling awareness was attached to a thread that went all the way back in time to the impact of early childhood. One just had to follow the feeling and see where it landed. We like to say that our feelings are like sausages in a string, and that

137

they are similar impacts of events that are connected. We could call this a *feeling memory string.*

Often, the early childhood memory in this feeling memory string was completely surprising to the person as the details of the event in childhood would be completely unrelated to the details of the person's present life issue that was the trigger of the feelings. But if they focused on the feelings, it was clear that the issue was the same in childhood as it was in the present and the person was often still trying to work out this issue in the present, an issue that began so very long ago.

Using the head brain alone (without gut feelings) to think back to earlier childhood did not access new memories. But feeling back in time, particularly centering on gut feelings of emptiness and fullness, would take people back to feelings in relation to events in their pasts that they had not previously remembered. This was usually true in each successive session using the Somatic Reflection Process. The common response after these somatic reflections was amazement at remembering things they had not previously remembered and how useful it was in giving them new insights and perspectives into the present adult issue and decision they may be facing.

How this occurs, that is, how or why neurologically the gut feeling is the key to recovering memory, we never knew when we first developed and used the process in the 70s. We just knew that it worked and that it helped people to resolve issues they had been carrying all their lives and that the acquired knowledge of self through this somatic process on gut feelings encouraged positive adult decision-making.

The Value of the Somatic Reflection Process in Recovering Feeling Memories

Although the details of our early lives do often come to our consciousness as a result of somatic reflection, the value in doing the inner work of reflecting on our gut feelings to recall our early childhood is not so we can remember these details — where we went on vacations as children or what we did there, the names of our childhood friends, the color of the walls of our childhood bedrooms, or our favorite tree house. But what is important is that our somatic reflections assist us in remembering the impact of life upon us, how it felt, what excited us in life and had value to us, how it felt to be loved or alone or confined or free, what decisions we made about our world and certainly most importantly was what we decided as children about ourselves and who we decided that we were or were not. When we remember through our feeling awareness these things, then we have valuable information that is the blueprint for making successful life-decisions as adults.

Since we primarily worked with adults, we have only some informal experience with the use of the Somatic Reflection Process with children below the age of 10 years old. So we do not know what the youngest age is that it would be useful to use to explore memory. We suspect that reflecting on gut feelings with young children as young as six or seven years old would be the key to educating the body-mind, our multiple brains, whole person, and to developing Intuitional Intelligence at an early age.

We do know that if used with adults to recover childhood memories, the Somatic Reflection Process on gut feelings is

139

both a key to and validates the recent findings that children do have the ability to form memories and that these memories are formed around the impact of their experience rather than around the details in their lives, a bottom-up rather than top-down formation. We also know that these memories are recoverable and the consciousness of them is valuable, perhaps even essential to good emotional and physical health and longevity.

It is also important to add that over the years, we have been successfully using the Somatic Reflection Process (SRP) on gut feelings to help people to unite body-mind. Often, and to their surprise, the people who experienced severe child abuse found that by using this process they were able to recover buried memories of bonding with parents. Even just one memory of bonding, of an experience of being loved by one's estranged parent, no matter how short, can make a big impact and go a long way toward giving strength to and healing the self-esteem and suffering of a person who feels they were never loved by their abusive parent. More on this in our next chapter on healing from child abuse

Using Gut Feelings to Heal From The Impact of Child Abuse

We offer this discussion on healing from child abuse in hopes to encourage anyone who has gone through this disturbance to seek help. We have had many case studies of people who were able to successfully begin the healing process from child abuse using the Somatic Reflection Process and we hope that sharing one with you will be of some benefit.

Child abuse often begins in the earliest years of our lives, prior to school age, even in our infancy. But try as we may, we cannot seem to find access to all of these very early memories (sometimes none at all) by simply thinking back in time to a very young age. Yet it is these horrific events of child abuse in our early lives that are still affecting us today in our feelings and perspectives, and even our lifestyle and decision-making. Often we experience feelings of guilt, shame, fear, and anger, as our feeling memories of child abuse are triggered in the present and current events of our lives. Therefore, in the present adult life, we often see our lives and ourselves through the lens of a child experiencing this abuse and we interpret our relationships with others in the present time from the view of that old perspective.

All of us want to be cleared of these difficult lingering feeling so we may be more in the now, experience peace and happiness, and make healthy life decisions. But how do we begin the healing process if thinking reflection—just thinking back in time—is not enough to uncover these memories? If you guessed the answer is in the awareness of the feelings in your gut, then you have certainly been paying attention to your reading of this book and are correct!

The following paragraph gives an example of this healing process for a person having experienced severe child abuse. We have case after case of memories of people that we sat with in counseling for hours exploring their past on a gut feeling level, but this one with Jim (his real name is protected although he gave us permission to write about him) will stay in our conscious memory forever.

Jim was an adult male in his early 30s and had experienced severe child abuse from a very early age until he left his family of origin as a teen. However, he had no conscious memories of his childhood before age six, when his family moved and he began grade school. He was working with us on the issue in his present life concerning being a single father of two young children and the emotional difficulties he was having in fulfilling his role as a father. He felt overwhelmed, to say the least. The dominant emotion he experienced was one of guilt, the guilt that he was not being a good enough parent. Sadness, fear and depression followed this dominant feeling of guilt. And below those feelings was a great emptiness and aloneness that he felt in his gut, a feeling he described as "like being down in an empty pit with no energy to climb out". We took that feeling awareness and gradually had him go back in time to see where he had felt that way before. He began remembering, uncovering, memories he had not had since the time he had the original experiences in childhood.

Within an hour of somatic reflection on gut feelings (time feels very quick when you are in this process of feeling memory), Jim was back remembering being three years old. As he accessed feeling memories at that time in his life, he was flooded with details of his life that he had completely forgotten, even the color of the walls in his room. But most importantly, while he remembered being abused, he was also able to understand some of his own behavior and see that he was successful in protecting himself and surviving the experience.

He had never seen that part of himself nor gave himself that credit. His feelings shifted in his body from feeling empty and depressed to empowered and energized. You can actually see this shift in a person when they make it. As counselors, we knew healing was beginning for Jim. He was able to use this new information of the strength of his survival to deal with the present issue and successfully fulfill his role as a single father. Jim had come to the important understanding (both in a feeling and core belief of self) that he was a "Survivor" and he could use this knowledge for strength in the present.

We did not find in counseling that all people uncovered the same message as Jim had when going through the Somatic Reflection Process on gut feelings, but it was often true of people who had experienced severe child abuse. Although for both those who did and who did not experience child abuse, the feeling awareness and memory recovered through this process is seen in the light and wisdom of an adult for the first time. This allows the person to be able to update his or her understanding of self from what was originally thought and held onto as an innocent young child who would not have enough information to see that they were not to blame for the problems in their lives, and certainly not for any abuse inflicted upon them.

We have often used the analogy in our counseling of having a hurtful pimple to having these unconscious memories of child abuse and accompanying emotions that are making our lives unhappy, and are in some way feeling as if they are controlling us. Once the pimple comes to a head and the infection comes out in full, healing occurs. But it all must come out before complete healing can take place. Similarly, once a childhood memory of abuse is fully conscious, brought into the daylight so to speak, the feeling impact of the experience changes (shifts) and emotional healing may begin.

There are layers and layers of unconscious memories, so for healing to take place we must be patient and take the time, often years, of inner work to be sure all the feeling memories are no longer buried in our consciousness. But working through feeling awareness on a gut level can render some very important healing results quickly, sometimes within a couple of hours. And we have never had anyone express that the process was painful, rather people feel that their inner needs are being met for the first time.

We do hope you will feel encouraged to find the right person to work with to access your feelings in the gut region of your body, and bring your memories to the light (whether you have experienced child abuse or not), find the inner child who has always guided you to survive, and feel the beauty of your Being. Your gut feelings are there for more than you may know and are the key to knowing your true self and for healing.

The Therapeutic Process in Psychotherapy and Accessing Gut Feelings

If a connectedness with another Human Being is either never adequately there for an infant in the beginnings of life or if this connection is broken by a traumatic experience in childhood,
then the healing process of the individual must provide this bonding experience with another Human being, such as a therapist who gives profound empathic understanding to a patient. The following chapter explores how through the therapeutic relationship, healing takes place and health is restored.

We also explore the literature that supports caring for the instinctive needs of Acceptance and Freedom and of the Somatic Reflection Process that we developed to assist people to feel into their gut feelings to access past experiences in the therapeutic process.

A large body of literature from Transpersonal Psychology, Humanistic Psychology, Object Relations, Self Psychology, Developmental Psychology, and Depth Psychology agree that the feeling of connectedness with another Human being is crucial to the therapeutic process and at the heart of the healing process. The element of connectedness realized in the healing process is viewed as necessary because Human beings learn who they are with the help of another.

Modern neuropsychological studies have shown that the thinking brain is developed with the aid of early stimulation. A child's experiences, influence the wiring of his/her brain and the connection in his/her nervous system. Attachment and loving interactions with caring adults stimulate a child's brain and cause synapses to grow and existing connections to get stronger, even become permanent. On the other hand, if a person receives little stimulation in early childhood, the synapses will not develop, which hampers the development of the brain and its learning connections. In this case, the CNS and the ENS also have fewer connections and there is a split in mind/body consciousness.

In the field of Transpersonal Psychology, Wittine recognizes the acceptance of another Human being as fundamental to the process of healing. In *Assumptions of Transpersonal Psychotherapy* he states that "The healing process is only possible when the client's true nature is recognized by the therapist. . . ." (p. 169). He goes on to say that through eyes that are unconditionally loving and accepting, the therapist must view the "inner light and beauty, creativeness, power, and dignity" of the client if healing is to occur. This quality of caring is similar to what Carl Rogers calls *unconditional positive regard*, the non judgmental

146

acceptance and empathy of one Human being for another, which requires "no gratification" on the part of the one caring. Wittine views the healing of the self as only being possible through the mirroring of another self, which is similar to the ideas of Object Relations and Self Psychology theorists concerning self-object experience and mirroring.

In the 60s, an English pediatrician and psychoanalyst Donald W. Winnicott postulated in *The Theory of the Parent-Infant Relationship* that the developing self of the infant and young child can only thrive in a nurturing environment with a mother or primary care giver. He views mental illness as a result of early failure of the environment to provide nurturing that is adaptable to the changing needs of the child.

Winnicott coined the phrase *good enough mother* to imply that there is a burden on the mother to provide an environment in which the child can develop an authentic sense of self, and the awareness true inner feelings. He posits that the good enough mother does not have to be perfect but does have to provide for the needs of the child most of the time. He further states in *The Theory of the Parent-Infant Relationship* that the infant must feel a sense that its spontaneous expressions of its needs are effective. The infant must feel "seen or understood to exist by someone" and the infant must "get back (as a face seen in a mirror) the evidence" of being "recognized as a being." This process is similar to what Heinz Kohut termed *mirroring* and we will be discussing this at length later.

Winnicott found that most of the people who came to him for help felt empty and ineffective because they had not been mirrored as infants by their caregiver. He found that people had created a false self and were reacting compliantly to the demands of the environment, that is, to the desires and

147

responses of other people. The false self had hidden the true self—the authentic self—and people therefore could not act spontaneously or genuinely. They had not developed an authentic sense of self, and were not able to express their own needs in relationships with others.

In *From dependence to independence in the development of the individual,* Winnicott views the relationship between the therapist and the patient as a replay of the person's relationship with their first caregiver, usually the mother. *In Playing and Reality,* he sees the therapeutic environment as a facilitating environment in which the therapist provides a safe container for the patient to grow in, which adapts to the needs of the client, and which fosters an emerging self-awareness. In that way, the therapist and patient assume the roles of mother and child and recreate a facilitating environment.

In Heinz Kohut's Self Psychology, the nurturing environment of the child is viewed as vital for healthy psychological growth. He views the importance of the nurturing environment to help the child know itself through the assistance of another, its primary care giver. Discussing his concept called *mirroring* in *The Restoration of the Self,* Kohut says that the infant looks to the mother and sees its own self reflected "in her happy gaze". Psychiatrist and Jungian analyst Lionel Corbett postulates in *The Religious Function of the Psyche* that if this does not occur, then "painful feelings of fragmentation, emptiness, depletion, unreality or hopelessness" result, along with a chronic emotional deficiency. Kohut calls this an empty self and views Human suffering as stemming from a lack of positive mirroring, which causes a sense of incompleteness in the person and feelings of emptiness and hopelessness.

We might postulate from the literature we have just cited that points to the need for both mirroring and empathy, that Human beings universally need to be witnessed and mirrored; and that this is only obtained through interaction with other people. Sharing similar feelings around a set of circumstances or shared images is one way for people to know that they experience their inner self in a similar way to other individuals.

In her book *Descent to the Goddess*, Jungian analysts Sylvia Brinton Perera combines the need for mirroring and the need for empathy when she describes empathic mirroring as an experience that two individuals have as they "share one psychic reality". During the experience of empathic mirroring, there is an awareness that both people share affect and image as if they are one person. It is through the experience of empathic mirroring that people obtain the information to know that they are members of the Human family; this gives them a deep sense of belonging. This sense of belonging obtained from mirroring is a stage toward positive ego development. If this mirroring experience is insufficient in childhood, people are left with doubts as to who they are, and they feel empty and alone inside. They may disconnect from the feelings of their true self, to adapt to others.

Fortunately, mirroring can occur as a healing process anytime in life. Adults can obtain the empathy that they need to feel full, complete, and integrated as members of the Human family.

Healing the Body/Psyche Link

We would like to bring to your attention some of the findings of those who have developed therapeutic processes with some similarity to the Somatic Reflection Process on gut feelings. It is

149

useful to review these findings because they have found as we have that the key to recovering memory and uniting the body/mind split is through reflection upon feelings in the body in early childhood.

In the 70s, Janoe and Janoe created an early recollection technique that they first used in a counseling process with elementary school children. The technique was used to reflect upon difficult feelings and started with locating an uncomfortable feeling in the body and centering on that feeling while recollecting memories from the past that felt the same.

The Janoes' model of integrating early recollections and body awareness restored a missing cognitive awareness, and their clients were often able to experience instant relief from what had initially seemed like free-floating anxiety. Because the recollection experience is a felt experience, the Janoes view this new perspective around stored memory to change the linkage between the "rational, body, and emotional selves, which are not be thought of as separate..." The Janoes believe that all feelings originate in childhood and are felt again by the person when he/she faces similar situations in the present.

Janoe and Janoe state in Dealing With Feelings Via Real Recollections, which was published in H. A. Olson's *Early recollections: Their use in diagnosis and psychotherapy*, that their recollection process is only to be used with learned feelings rather than feelings with an organic cause. In early childhood, an experience that a person responds to directly is stored as a feeling in the body. Although not conscious of the original source of the stored memory, the body responds with the same feeling to a similar experience in the present as was felt in the original experience.

This process of reflecting upon the feeling experience and then tracing it back to the original experience allows the person to feel the original experience and rethink the need to keep the original feeling reaction in the present. The person can see that what once was a viable feeling reaction that made good sense at the time, may not be necessary in the present. Janoe and Janoe stress the importance of connecting the original feeling experience stored in the body to the present thinking capacities of the person who is older, and who may now elect to choose a response that is more appropriate.

In 2004, an exploration of this model by Adlerian psychologists Disque and Bitter further revised the Janoes' method for use with people who have suffered trauma. Disque and Bitter include the technique of asking the person to remember the moment before the memory or trauma and to experience the feeling of well-being they had in that previous moment. The person reflecting is instructed to walk into the memory with this strength and centeredness of the earlier moment.

In the *Journal of Individual Psychology*, in an article titled Emotion, Experience, and Early Recollections: Exploring Restorative Reorientation Processes in Adlerian Therapy, Disque and Bitter's hypothesis that the sense of well-being of the previous moment before an experience helps people to remember and reassess the experience rather than just relive it. The hope of using Janoes' process with persons who have experienced childhood trauma is that they are able to reassess the meaning of experience from an adult view rather than a child's view and perceive the situation with greater clarity.

Instincts Reflected as Archetypal Symbols

Perhaps it would be easier to be mindful of our bodies, and we would more willingly become focused on our inner experience as a guide in our lives, if we knew what we would discover about our instincts once we followed them. If we want to understand our Human instincts, we need only to turn to the awareness of archetypes. Carl Jung describes these archetypes as primordial, inborn forms or patterns that we encounter in our psyche, both individually and collectively. Archetypes operate at the deep level of the instincts and can affect both body and mind.

According to Jung, archetypes are experienced in all of Humanity and are the primary component of the collective unconscious. The collective unconscious is a part of the psyche that does not owe its existence to personal experience but rather to heredity. Jung views the deepest level of instinctual wisdom as capable of being reached only by the awareness of the symbol of an archetype, which he regards as "the instinct's perception of itself, or as the self-portrait of the instinct" (see *The concept of the collective unconscious, Collective Works*, Volume 9). He considers instincts as having inherent goals, with archetypes mirroring to us our instincts. Because archetypes are a reflection of instincts, they affect energies that influence our bodies.

The late Depth Psychologist Joseph L. Henderson was able to sift through the many archetypal symbols of mythology and see a pattern running through all mythological stories of the ancient struggle between containment and liberation. In Ancient Myths and Modern Man (see *Man and His Symbols,* he describes the common theme of the hero who first must leave the stable and contained environment of home to go on a lonely journey. By leaving the life in which a person has enjoyed security to go into the wilderness alone, the hero is seeking liberation or release. At the moment that we break all ties of containment and bring ourselves to face new discoveries or live in a new way, we are seeking liberation. According to Henderson, Dante's dream of *The Divine Comedy* symbolizes liberation in his journey to hell, purgatory, and heaven. Mythological stories with themes concerning the "conflict between adventure and discipline, evil and virtue, or freedom and security" (p. 157) are all concerned with the Human struggle between the need for containment and liberation. A well known example in mythology is the Greek god Hermes. He was a messenger and god of the crossroads leading "souls to and from the underworld" (p. 156), and symbolized moving from the known to the unknown—from containment to liberation.

Although the details of the mythological stories have changed throughout history, Henderson points out that the underlying, archetypal themes and psychic meanings have not changed and that we continue to express a cultural unconscious. Ancient symbols of containment, like the Great Mother, that once symbolized stability and protection, are now replaced by modern Humankind's search for economic security and social welfare. Ancient mythological symbols like the winged dragon, winged horse, bird, or serpent that symbolized the search for liberation, are replaced today by the images of jet planes and space rockets. Henderson's observations in *Thresholds of Initiation,* on the mythic structure of the hero, point to a dynamic struggle of mankind to balance containment and liberation.

We see a strong correlation between these instincts that Henderson sees—containment (symbolized by the mother image of birth and love) and liberation (symbolized by the freedom of air travel)—and the gut instincts that we have found using the Somatic Reflection Process: the need for acceptance for who we are naturally (attention from a caring Human) and control of one's own responses (freedom to respond naturally).

Holding the Tension of Opposites and Self-Regulation

It is our experience that our instinctual needs of acceptance (attention) and control (freedom) are compensatory in that one need flows into the other. While they may not both be met at the same time (and we often have to give up one for the other, at least temporarily), they must be met in some balance for the Human Being to feel full of life and vitality. So let us look a minute at how the Human psyche holds opposites in a self-regulatory pattern.

We know that even though we may not be aware of our struggles with holding the tension of opposites, our unconscious takes on the task. Carl Jung saw the human psyche as self-regulatory and the tension of opposites within us holds the key to this self-regulation process. Just as the Human body self-regulates, so does the Human psyche. The Human body, for instance, will sweat to cool off the body during high temperatures and thus self-regulate.

The Human psyche will self-regulate through dreams that bring to our consciousness the awareness of our inner truth. An example of this self-regulation would be for the highly
154

intellectual person who is not conscious of their feelings to have very emotional dreams. Jungians often see nightmares as reflecting controlled emotions in our day (conflicting aspects of ourselves) and as compensatory dreams for the purpose of self-awareness and self-regulation.

Swiss Jungian Psychologist Jolande Jacobi, in *The Psychology of C.G. Jung*, suggests that the unconscious hears the voice of our primal nature without the influence of the environment or the conscious goals of the ego (p. 35). She further sees its purpose is to oppose all one-sidedness of the ego that might lead us down the road to isolation. For example, if we are strongly identified with our persona (the face we show the world), then our shadow elements of ourselves will emerge in our dream content.

Have you ever wondered what the meaning of your dreams are when they seem so unlike what you think or feel is going on in your life? It may well be the unconscious helping to bring to your awareness both the light and dark within, your inner truth. This is often true when you have a very positive dream during a stressful period in your life or a disturbing dream when you think you are on top of the world. Jung describes in *Transformations and Symbols of the Libido* this process of bringing to our awareness the balance of both the light and dark within us as the *compensatory nature of the unconscious*. The purpose of the unconscious is to direct us toward wholeness through the urge to individuate, and to balance the pole of opposites within us by holding the tension between them.

Jacobi further asserts that there is a law of opposition in the nature of the psyche that keeps intact an inner self-regulation system. Everything within the unconscious must ultimately flow into its opposite, causing a re-evaluation of earlier values.

155

Heraclitus called this return to the opposite *enantiodromia*. Jacobi sees that it is in the depths of introversion that the psyche may experience this "spontaneous reversal of libido" (p. 54), where energy is transformed from one pole of opposites to another. When the conscious mind expresses itself with one value, it will come to an extreme where the unconscious will compensate with the opposite value. Jung viewed the experience of holding the tension that exists between the opposites as the key to wholeness.

We can see the enantiodromia effect occurring as the individual becomes aware of gut feelings and instinctual needs—as we move naturally to fulfill a balance of acceptance and freedom in our lives.

Balancing the Two Instinctual Needs— Acceptance and Freedom to Respond Naturally

The father of Humanistic Psychology Carl Rogers points out in *On Becoming a Person: A therapist's view of psychotherapy* the importance of the individual having the freedom to respond naturally and authentically as one truly feels inside, rather than as one perceives one should or should not respond in relation to the demands of others. His view is that as people become more aware of how they naturally feel and who they really are from an inner awareness of value and feeling, they find that they have more choices available to them, and they begin to appreciate their own capabilities and potentials. In becoming more aware of who we really are, we experience inner freedom, and Rogers identifies this as primarily a *fully functioning person*. In his work, *A Theory of therapy, personality, and interpersonal relationships, as developed in the client-centered framework,* Roger's describes a fully functioning person as feeling inwardly free to move in any direction, and thus is self-directing. With a higher sense of self direction, the person becomes more self confident and takes the responsibility to direct one's own life.

Object Relations and Self Psychologists point to the Human lifetime occupation with achieving both acceptance and freedom. They identify the importance of the experience of the child with internalized relations of self objects so the child can obtain the needs of mirroring and idealizing. Donald Winnicott, suggests that a facilitating environment is nurturing when it both provides mirroring and adapts to the changing responses of the child. The need for mirroring and idealizing points to the instinctual need of the child for acceptance. The adapting, responsive quality of the facilitating environment points to the need of the child to have the freedom to respond naturally and experience a sense of internal control rather than external control.

It is both important for the child to receive mirroring for a sense of belonging to occur and also to experience the attention of the caregiver as responsive to the their feelings. If a caregiver allows the child the freedom to respond naturally but does not attend the child with ample mirroring, the child may feel neglected and alone. If a caregiver is attentive but does not take into account the child's inner feelings and changing needs, the child may feel controlled and smothered by this attention. This supports the importance of the careful balancing of the two needs of acceptance and freedom of one's own responses for the health of the developing psyche and is important to consider in parenting styles and in the educational process.

157

Part 4

How the Consciousness of the Gut as a Brain Affects Religion and Culture

Social Problem Solving with Instinctual Awareness

On these next few pages, we give a final word about the old model of thinking of our Human Nature as centered around having only one-brain. We summarize our work on the importance of favoring a two-brain image and the meaning of this new image as insight into social problem solving that will guide Humanity into the next step in benevolent cultural evolution as we honor our instincts and develop our Intuitional Intelligence.

In recorded Human history, cultures have seldom if ever to our knowledge demonstrated evidence of dependable Human behavior with their model of one center of intelligence in the head. Because of the over-dominance of the head brain and suppression of the gut instincts (which are necessary for self-regulation), there has throughout modern recorded history been a required powerful center of intelligence from an external source (religious and civil laws) to guide people to attempt to produce constant, dependable and acceptable social behavior.

We have presented a functional image of a two-brain model that suggests that there is a dynamic learning experience of the available instincts at birth, which is combined with the emerging developing main sensory brain and must work with new sensory data from the environments into which it is thrust throughout its life. We postulate that such learning experiences from birth on through early developing childhood can produce a dependable problem-solving skill. It can produce an emerging intuition that will mature over time to serve the organism throughout its life (depending on the quality of the diverse environments it encounters). When such an intuition matures, it could furnish the Human with directions to achieve the best possible pathway toward the greatest satisfaction in life for itself—with a minimum of authoritative external social control of any kind.

The idea of taking on a social enterprise and consciously using only the present image of Human Nature—a single center of intelligence capable of both good and evil that requires an external power of control to minimize evil behavior and maximize good behavior—seems never to have completely solved any cultural Human need in Human history. In spite of this record of failure for thousands of years, that is the primitive image we are still using and it is full of misunderstandings. This works to direct our decisions toward external solutions that lead us away from Human inner necessities. The little accuracy we have in the use of our logic system alone when making personal and cultural decisions rarely provides Human and cultural need satisfaction. This has left Humans today, through following this one-brain concept of self, feeling empty and confused.

The use of that primitive model has certainly been excusable in the past, since Human behavior could only be observed from an external frame of reference and our minds are still functioning based on that experience. External behavior does not necessarily reveal the inner purpose of the expended

162

Human energy within, and it may only reveal the use of the single, thinking brain working well with things in the outside world—Human development of tools and things leading up to the Industrial Revolution whether necessary or not.

We must realize, however, that Human Nature has been furnishing the energy to that upper brain, which can produce only external stature and safety for the temporary, external and cultural satisfaction and it can give little internal satisfaction to Human Nature's internal needs. Inner dissatisfaction is now being expressed around the world by the masses as they realize they are loosing their share of return for the Human energy expended. **There are important inner needs missing from the Human diet beside food, air, water, and money to make life worth living.** We have labored to produce energy to sustain the culture and sustain ourselves but our inner nature requires its Freedom and Acceptance as individuals for our efforts—life processes, intuitive actions and healthy environments.

To further complicate matters and make it difficult to embrace a new experience and model of Self and others, far more fibers carry information processed by the higher area of the Human cortex down to the lower regions of the cortex than the sensory information being carried up to the higher regions. The result of this nearly one-way feedback system in the cortex is that we generally see what we already believe, hear what we expect to hear, and have a difficult time ever having a new experience or beginner's mind. Sounds as if it is easy for our beliefs to become a bit stale, doesn't it! According to authors Sandra and Matthew Blakeslee in their book *The Body Has a Mind of Its Own* (2007), this explains why our reality is constructed in a large way according to our expectations and beliefs and holds the key to why it is hard to change one's body image.

With the upper cortex dominating our perception and flood of sensory information over our inner awareness of body sensation and feelings, we are losing the special attention to the gut feeling signals and the awareness of these important gut feelings. This also explains the mechanism of internal disconnects between the two intelligence centers (thinking head brain and gut brain). This disconnect deprives us of our needed personal directions and causes us to experience an unhealthy amount of stress symptoms.

> "By letting go of what is known, you are free to encounter the living present, in all its perplexity and revelation."
> —Philip Shepherd in *New Self, New World: Recovering Our Senses in the Twenty-First Century*

We would suggest that our dilemma of present social problem-solving, particularly the problems concerning the governing of Human beings, is a sign of not using an accurate functional (usable) image of Human Nature. A new image is required for direction, confidence, and final assurance that our directions into the future are relevant to individual Human needs. These new directions must have the support of what we now know of Nature's Ways—natural forces, internal and external, must be considered to optimize life.

If we think for a moment about how we are making decisions individually and collectively, we realize that we are working backwards in our problem solving. We have ignored the

164

Reverence for Life revered by Albert Schweitzer (1936). With only external objectives in mind, we argue about our Human differences not realizing that in many respects we each have the same inner Human need for control (freedom) and acceptance (attention), which sponsors co-operation. While arguing about external details, which are built on different environmental life experiences, tends to sponsor competition, it also has little to add to Human need satisfaction. With only conscious external objectives in our thinking and with little feeling for those who trusted us to represent them, we tend to end up talking past each other and without offering material satisfaction to life for ourselves and those for whom we have responsibility. We seem to be unable to consciously use the intelligence with which we were born—as though the instincts are for temporary use and only for the newborn, rather than for development throughout Human life and for being a necessity for wellness in aging.

Instinctual Aging For Wellness of Individual and Culture

The feeling responses of the gut can certainly be recognized by all Humans—empty or full— and the enteric nervous system (ENS) supports life processes whether or not there is conscious awareness of all its activities. This is especially true when the system needs food, water, air, or getting rid of waste products. The gut is dedicated to the well being of its genetic inheritance—especially its Instincts.

The instincts are the center of the organism's intelligence, which is what has been learned and stored by its experience in dealing with the multitude of variables of the upper brain (CNS), then passed along in the genes to future generations

165

over time as experience—new intelligence. This new intelligence will function as an additional future value to the intuition for problem-solving. By combining the conscious use of the instinctive feelings, the inner value to the needs of his-Self or her-Self, with the sensory experiences provided by the individual's unique environment, the individual prepares an optimum, more-healthy pathway to the future for Self and the culture. The environment must furnish some element of support of the inner basic needs. When these two centers of intelligence—the (ENS) and (CNS)—are working together in harmony, Self Control and Self Acceptance will have been learned by experience—experience that hopefully begins at birth—and instinctual aging will occur with greater satisfaction of Human needs that support a vibrant and healthy person and culture.

Was Religion Invented By the Thinking Mind to Try to Make Sense of Gut Feeling and Gut Instinct?

There are those who have said for some time that "God" speaks through the gut, the most natural part of us that can not be altered by the thinking brain. And now,

Nicolas Baumard of the University of Pennsylvania and Pascal Boyer of Washington University in St. Louis have recently added something new to the mix in their publication in the journal *Current Directions in Psychological Science*. They theorize that religious beliefs are a result of the thinking brain trying to explain gut feelings that are expressed in intuitive thought. According to Baumard and Boyer, religious beliefs originate in our initial intuitions about things that are completely unrelated to God, gods, and afterlife—intuitions that were at one time in Human existence adaptive, but no longer are adaptive or usable. These beliefs are not simply intuitions but are the deliberate logical brain's attempt to explain gut feelings we have about death and dying as we experience the loss of a loved one or fear of impending dangers.

It may be that Baumard and Boyer have come across the same thing that we have discovered in our work, that religion has historically been fortified by only one of our instinctual needs for a gut feeling experience of "connectedness" or acceptance. As we have emphasized throughout this book, religion at present does not completely explain the entire gut feeling experience and often sees gut instinct as disruptive to society. While religious doctrine may care about the gut instinctual need for acceptance (connection), it leaves out the gut instinctive need for freedom (a sense of control of one's own responses to life). As we have explained, we found in our work that our gut feelings express both of these needs and that we need them in balance—the need for acceptance (connectedness and attention) and the need for freedom (control of one's own responses). Leaving out in religious doctrine the importance of the Human need for freedom is a primary reason that religion often fails to be truly functional in supporting Human life. While fundamentalist religions may talk of supporting Free Will in humankind, Free Will is only acceptable if the person accepts the religious doctrines of a particular religion and there is no encouragement toward the importance of following one's true inner natural responses for a sense of control and freedom.

Perhaps what Baumard and Boyer are seeing is that we Humans have historically needed to find a way to feel safe and connected and have undoubtedly been willing to give up our instinctual need for freedom and to accept religious doctrine in order to experience this feeling of safety, containment, and acceptance. We could say, then, that it was what we needed most at the time that we accepted a religious doctrine. Although not completely satisfying, one of the two of our instinctive needs, acceptance/containment, was satisfied by joining this religious community and belief system. Perhaps acceptance was the one instinctual need most pressing at the time for our survival. And this lack of fulfillment of our instinctual need for freedom (a sense of control of our own responses to life) may explain why so many people feel that religion now leaves us empty and scratching our heads.

We view the present dissatisfaction with religion expressed by many people today as an indication that we are ready for a new image of Humanity, a new belief system about who we are and our relationship to the greater Universe that encompasses our need for freedom as well as it does our need for acceptance. The trick for our new 21st century spiritual belief system is to adapt one that assists us in feeling containment and acceptance as well as a sense of freedom and self-control.

We can see in a glimpse of history that religious beliefs have often in the past been contrived to control people from having a sense of individuality and to the advantage of someone or group outside of the individual person. These religious thoughts or beliefs are generally external to the understanding of the needs of the individual Human being. Gut feelings always reflect the instinctive needs of the Human being, while religious thought often will drown out our awareness of our gut feelings and needs in favor of following a doctrine.

"Learn from yesterday, live for today, hope for tomorrow. The important thing is to not stop questioning."
— Albert Einstein from *Relativity: The Special and the General Theory*

An important question here is, did the thinking brain, the CNS, come up with religious thought and beliefs to explain gut feeling and gut instinct (the ENS) or did it invent religious belief to control instinct? Or perhaps both are true? Is this invention of religious beliefs that do not consider humans as self-regulating or having self-control, a natural and common pattern of the CNS, an evolution of mind with further steps ahead? Or is this an unnatural turn in Human events that has been invented by only a few in history and then followed by billions. And perhaps we could say that this tendency to follow without question is also a necessary learning experience and therefore a natural step of Human evolution and intelligence. And if so, now that we have had this *trial and learning* period (over 2000 years now), Humans may have another step soon ahead that will be comprised of using what we have learned to demand less following and more individual expression and

169

freedom? Are we getting to the point in history where we as a Humanity are questioning these past "inventions of religious thought" and through somatic reflection on our inner truth are seeing a need for change? Perhaps we are only a few tiny steps away from being ready as a Humanity to accept a new image of Humanity that embraces both of our instinctive needs—our needs of acceptance and of freedom—and thus explains and helps us understand our connection to the Universe in ways that feel more truly Human and increases benevolent evolution.

The Gut as a Part of Mind

We have been asked by several of our readers of *What's Behind Your Belly Button?* to correlate our work with gut feeling intelligence located in the Hara and the healing the body-mind split to Buddhism and thoughts about Mind and the chakras system. This very short discussion briefly addresses that relationship.

Many people have asked us how our work relates to the Buddhist chakra system. Most Buddhist locate the Mind chakra above the navel rather than the navel itself. This focus is not at odds with our work concerning the navel area because the compassion of the heart (or any other higher chakra) can only be opened after the Hara—gut, navel chakra—is clearly conscious, the body-mind connection is in sync, and the body-mind split is healed.

In many ways, the Buddhist meditations we may participate in become much more accessible to us after doing the inner work using the Somatic Reflection Process on gut feelings to clear us of blockages in the gut region of the body. So, perhaps in more ways than not, we are on the same tract as Buddhist Psychology. Our difference, if there really is one and not just a difference in semantics, is that we suggest that the body "Is a part of Mind", at least while we are in it in this physical existence. And we view our lifetime purpose of bringing spirit into matter to require consciously feeling into the here and now through gut instinctual reflections and listening to the gut voice, which is a Western version of chakra meditation.

We do respect the heart as an intelligent center of compassion. However, as we have said earlier, we have felt that the heart has been given much of the credit for the intelligence of our consciousness that the gut intelligence gives us and this truly needs to be understood more accurately for the Human species to evolve into its highest potential of mind, both culturally and individually.

A Psychological View
of Redemption

In this essay, we discuss a scientific and psychological interpretation of the meaning of Redemption. We do this to give you a clear example of how the inclusion of the importance and awareness of Human Instincts in viewing religious and spiritual ideas changes our understanding of ourselves to be more useful to Human life and wellness.

It may be said that few of us really understand the deeper esoteric meaning of "redemption" and thus many people who speak of redemption—primarily in the Christian religion— simply understand it as some sort of higher spiritual external force granting forgiveness to a lost soul through some atonement. But as we become more aware of ourselves through reflection on our gut feelings and instincts, we understand redemption with more self-involvement. We then may redefine it in broader and more psychological and universal terms as a deep renewal process of returning to the true Self, the Source of our Being. We discover in that awareness the true Nature of the Human Being. For at the core of the Human Being, within all our Natures, springs our vital energy connected to the sacred. There within our Nature and instincts we find the impact of our experiences upon us, our truth as we know it, and the inner needs that flower our motivation behind all our actions. And with this inner awareness of Self, even those actions we find difficult to explain or understand in positive ways become clear as intentions of caring.

Without an awareness of our inner Nature, we have no truth to hold onto and little of what we think is actually real. But how can we say our past is not really what we think it is? How can we say that we have always cared as Human Beings in our guts and our Human Nature? How can we say this when there are actions we know we have committed that were vile and poisonous to others? And when there are actions we have not made that have left our brothers and sisters alone and cold? We know the history of our actions, our behavior, so how can we challenge that these hauntings we have—these thoughts of who we have been—are not real? The evidence weighs so very heavy in favor of focusing on the illusion of external beliefs of good and evil, and in believing that truth lies only in an external judgment of Human actions. And we are told to believe that the unseen part of the Human experience is best left described as the "beast" by many in the religious majority and that this beast must be tamed—a belief that is said to be "all a powerful instrument for Human mind control and a dogma that has become the foundation of Human behavior control in both Mid Eastern and Western cultures".

But what truly needs to be "tamed" for enlightenment to occur? Our inner Nature and instinct or our propensity of ignorance with a childlike innocence toward accepting the glamour of external judgments and thinking about ourselves? In reflection of our past, what part of us really got us in trouble? Our instinctive needs or our acceptance of inaccurate thinking about ourselves? Was our fear born out of an instinctive Human need or a negative view, an illusion, we accepted quite early in life about the lack of divinity of our true selves? Did we then behave in less than caring ways due to our fears? And like a snowball rolling down a hill, did we compound those actions

173

based on our illusions until it was so big that we lost site of where it all began, how it all began, why it all began?

True redemption can only come once we lose our understanding of the truth of where we have come from and what we have truly needed. Only then are we compelled from our suffering to reflect upon our lives to understand how our inner needs are so vastly different from what we have accepted from the external judgments and views upon us that have been inaccurate descriptions of our core being. We then see that what we think was reality was not. When the whole picture of who we have been is revealed, then we understand the confusion in our awareness of ourselves and can distinguish for the first time the "me" and the "not me". Those old tapes of beliefs about self and others, and those emotional hauntings that we have been running over and over and feeding energy into with our every action, begin to fade away into oblivion.

The truth of Self is our strongest energy on earth and has the ability to erase the past, the past that we thought was true, the past that we have suffered thinking was all that there was in our life history, in our Human Nature, in the very core of our being. That false and unholy past is erased for the truth turns on all the lights within us at last, our fear is gone, and we feel only eternal peace at the core of our caring nature. We step into the awareness of being a part of the Human Family, home at last in this connection. It is there that we find each other, there that we join in doing what we as Humans are meant to do, and there that history pivots in an eternal reality.

Part 5

How Uniting our Multiple Brains Affects Health and Wellness, and the Medical Profession

Instinctual Awareness and Personalized Medicine

The following chapter describes the importance in aging and longevity of developing ones instinctual awareness and ability to fulfill inner needs. We also take a look at Personalized Medicine and suggest the Somatic Reflection Process as an intervention modality to be used for certain genetic diseases that have been found to have specific personality traits associated with them that also relate to our instinctual needs, as well as to be used for general preparation for the experience of aging with wellness.

The importance of recent longevity studies—some of which we have discussed earlier in this book—is in their impact on Personalized Medicine. In the last few years Functional Medicine that emphasizes using an integrative model with a patient-centered rather than disease-centered approach to treatment, has taken the holistic approach a step further. Now we see emerging Personalized Medicine, with the goal of giving primary care with preventative treatments based on individual patient differences, including not just age and the conditions of disease, but of genetic makeup. If a disease runs in your family and is found in your specific genetic makeup, then preventive medicine of that particular disease can be administered. The hope of Personalized Medicine is that a personalized lifestyle plan that would include nutritional needs as well as psychological needs specific to your genomic data would be prescribed to individuals.

Thanks to longevity studies correlating disease, mortality rates and personality traits, intervention modalities in Personalized Medicine can now target assessed personality traits related to ones genetic makeup. It is important to identify those personality traits that are considered risky for certain diseases and for diseases of aging. By studying what personality traits are most experienced in those living long lives and also those traits that are risk-prone for disease or early aging, personality phenotype for longevity is now possible to be integrated into Personalized Medicine and to disease preventive approaches. For instance, we know that a lower neuroticism is important for managing stress and this affects certain diseases and longevity. So modalities that help lower stress (like mindfulness techniques and the Somatic Reflection Process) are helpful in lowering neuroticism and thus are important to enhance wellness and longevity, particularly for those with high levels of neuroticism. This type of tailor made treatment planning enhances the probability of successful medical care. It is our hope that psychologists and physicians will work together to provide a personalized wellness program to patients that will include the use of the Somatic Reflection Process to assist people in honing their instincts to develop desired personality traits for a long and healthy life.

Another example of the positive influences of both Personalized Medicine and Functional Medicine is that patients may be taken in a case-by-case basis for certain important

178

medical care that would not have happened as a general rule in the past. We know for a fact that person-centered medicine rather than disease-centered medicine is trending because one of the authors of this book is 96 years old and is currently recovering from a knee replacement. And we might add that it took him two years of commitment to following his own instincts and being persistent in searching for a surgeon that would perform this surgery on him despite his chronological age. According to *The Journal Arthritis Care & Research* (August 2007), giving a centenarian knee surgery is quite uncommon and is still today in 2015 considered to be too risky by many surgeons. However now, considering the individual's physical health and genetic factors along with one's social environment and support, as well as one's personality traits, there are some progressive medical groups that do perform selective surgeries not done previously upon centenarians and 90-somethings. With increasing amounts of people becoming centenarians, it is important that the field of Medicine urges that elective surgery should not be deferred, particularly if it will enhance motility. Nor should emergency surgery be denied to the centenarian on the basis of chronologic age alone.

From recent longevity studies cited in *The Journal of Aging Research* in 2012 by authors Benjamin P. Chapman, Brent Roberts, and Paul Duberstein, we have summarized on the next page the significant characteristics positively affecting longevity. We have divided them into two areas, those that relate to the instinctual need for acceptance from others (attention), and those that relate to the instinctual need to be in control of one's own responses to life (freedom).

LONGEVITY TRAITS THAT RELATE TO THE DEVELOPED AWARENESS OF THE INSTINCTUAL NEED FOR ACCEPTANCE (ATTENTION):

- **High Extroversion** (It involves the tendency toward positive mood, sociability, and much social interaction. It is also associated with looking after yourself—with high self-acceptance—as a positive trait for longevity)
- **Lower Levels of Neuroticism** (It involves less chronic experience of specific negative emotions such as anxiety, depression, and anger, with a high sense of sociability. Social interaction is highly beneficial to longevity.)
- **Agreeableness and Easygoingness** (These relate to maintaining interpersonal harmony, like trust, honesty and compassion for others.)

LONGEVITY TRAITS THAT RELATE TO THE INSTINCTUAL NEED TO BE IN CONTROL OF ONE'S OWN RESPONSES TO LIFE:

- **Conscientiousness** (It involves a strong self-regulatory—self-discipline—component and relates to self-care. See The Longevity Project.)
- **High sense of coherence** (It involves perceptions of control over one's life and adaptation to hardship or life challenges.)
- **Openness to Experience** (It involves cognitive and behavioral flexibility.)

At a glance, you can see that with experience in using our instincts to fulfill ourselves in relation to our social needs and in having experience using our instincts to feel in control of our responses to life, we can achieve these important personality traits listed for wellness and longevity. The Somatic Reflection Process is suggested as a modality to use to enhance these desired personality traits. The results of using it have been reported in research and our clinical use with hundreds of people to be: 1. Increased Somatic Awareness: Feeling better in their bodies as a result of the reflection work and being more aware than before of what their bodily feelings are. 2. Increased Insights: Viewing a new way to perceive unresolved life problems or inner issues they were struggling with in the present and having an increased ability to identify inner needs and awareness of the need for acceptance (attention) and control (freedom) 3. And an increased feeling of self-acceptance (including dealing with fears, accepting one's need for others, and feeling happy).

We recommend using the Somatic Reflection Process to find the source of inner personal conflicts and resolving issues beginning in early childhood when instinctual awareness was first diminished. We recommend this modality for anyone who has an issue in self-acceptance (and thus meeting ones social needs) as well as those feeling out of control in their present condition and needing a hopeful and insightful perception of self and others to increase their sense of freedom and need for mobility.

How Doctors Can Save Lives by Listening to their Gut Feelings During a Diagnosis

This is written specifically for physicians. It is hoped that at some time in the near future, formal experimentation will occur using the Somatic Reflection Process to assist doctors in early training to learn better to access their gut feelings to be used as important data in diagnosis. This is an example of the importance of instinctual awareness in the development of Intuitional Intelligence that may save many lives.

A recent study at the University of Oxford has found that doctors who experience a gut feeling when treating a child should not ignore it. The Oxford study found that serious infections can be easily missed in young children and that a doctor's intuitive feeling that something is wrong, even after an examination suggests otherwise, appears to have even greater diagnostic value than most signs and symptoms. This large study was conducted on over 3000 children visiting their primary care Physician in Flanders, Belgium, in 2004 and it demonstrated the importance of gut feelings in medical diagnosis.

So why is this so? We thought we might explore this in terms of what we have found in our many years of working with people exploring gut feelings for decision-making. Of course the best exploration would be with doctors themselves and a little later in this essay we will suggest just such a study and exploration.

182

We know that gut feelings hold information about the impact of our life upon us and they are the key to our feeling memories and patterns of intuitive experiences. Gut feelings reveal our unconscious information and often this information comes to our awareness before conscious information in our thinking. Unconscious information is held in our bodies. That is why a painting we create today may hold clues to what we will consciously learn about ourselves in the future and that is the bases for exploring art as therapy and as a depth psychology process. Children are often not able to verbalize their feeling of trauma, but they can draw or do art about these feelings. Adults are really no different, although they may have learned some communication skills around feelings. It stands to reason that physicians would become aware of their unconscious accumulated information from past medical cases through their gut feelings long before the actual data for a conscious diagnosis becomes available to them.

As we previously discussed in an earlier chapter, we found in counseling that if a person reflects on their life by using their gut feelings of emptiness or fullness rather than just trying to think back about what happened (centering on details) and goes back in time using these feelings as a focus, they are surprised at the amount of data and information that also comes flooding in. They discover memories of details that they had buried in the unconscious and could not access through merely trying to think back to earlier times. Surely, this access to stored feeling memory is also the case for doctors and needs to be explored.

We thought it might be useful for doctors to have a personalized beginning of the protocol of the Somatic Reflection Process written specifically for their use while reflecting back on their gut feelings that prompt a curious look

183

into a gut feeling medical diagnosis. It would be interesting if doctors would take these gut feelings that they have about a diagnosis and reflect upon them, exploring them to more precisely uncover some patterns that they have in their unconscious signals concerning disease. Here is the beginning of a special demonstration of using the Somatic Reflection Process for physicians:

1. Center on the gut feeling about your patient. If you cannot locate this feeling at this time, then try to see the patient's face in your mind and say the diagnosis to your self. Now as you do this, begin to focus on your feelings in your body.

2. Now describe just that feeling in your body while you keep any details of the issue in your mind. Now express the feeling. (Studies on gut feelings during diagnosis have thus far shown doctors to have either a gut feeling with a sense of alarm that something does not fit or one of reassurance concerning the diagnosis.)

3. From here the physician will be able to use the general protocol of the Somatic Reflection Process (SRP) for exploring unresolved issues and life events (see page 155 of our book *What's Behind Your Belly Button?*). At this point, the reflection may take twists and turns into both the personal life and professional life of the physician and of seemingly unrelated events to the present situation and diagnosis. This guide will allow you to explore systematically your feeling memory and most likely see patterns you hold in your unconscious that are based on both life experience and your medical practice, with an increase of access to information stored in your unconscious.

The use of the Somatic Reflection Process by doctors with gut feeling diagnosis would make a very fascinating and potentially significant heuristic research study in itself. Doctors may be holding far more medical knowledge in their unconscious that has never fully surfaced than we might imagine. And we may also find that doctors who have skills in accessing their gut feelings in general in their personal lives, have an added diagnostic gut feeling ability in their medical professional practice. This could have implications for educational programs for the general practitioners to include teaching a process like the Somatic Reflection Process to enhance self-awareness of medical students.

Improving Gut Health Using the Somatic Reflection Process to Influence Both Physical and Mental Health

A discussion follows of how the Somatic Reflection Process on gut feelings may be helpful in both cell repair of the body and positive mental health. We propose that the Somatic Reflection Process be used along with "good" gut flora for health and wellness. The more a person uses the Somatic Reflection Process on gut feelings, the happier their gut becomes and this unites body and mind and allows positive signals to flow from gut to the head brain, improving mental and physical health.

*Y*ou have most likely read the latest news about a large study at a number of institutions, including UCLA, that link good gut health (including eating yogurt with probiotics daily) to affect brain functioning and to have positive affects upon mental health (study was with only women). For some time, scientists have understood how the head brain effects the gut in development. As early as the 1830's, William Beaumont, an army surgeon who is known now as the "Father of Gastric Physiology", found an association between changing moods and gastric secretions.

The classical view of top-down control with the head brain's ability to control gut function has been traditionally supported by evidence revealing that the brain influences body systems, like the gastro intestinal tract, particularly when the person is under stress. Now there is new evidence to show also that a bottom-up control with the gut, the microbiota in the gastro-intestinal tract, can influence head brain functioning and is linked to behavior, depression, stress, and stress-related diseases. Neuroscientists are now evaluating the role of gut microbiota modulation on emotional processing in the thinking brain and its functioning. This "good" bacteria—the beneficial flora in your gut—may be instrumental in how your brain develops, you behave, and react to stress.

We propose that there is much more you can do in addition to building up the good flora in your body to assure good gut health that effects positive mental health. Based on our clinical studies and research findings, we propose that the more a person uses the Somatic Reflection Process on gut feelings and unites body-mind, the happier their gut is, the more positive signals will flow from gut to head brain, and the person's mental health will be vastly improved. We also propose that

186

this use of this process causes an increase in stress reduction that has positive affects upon the physical body and the elimination of dis-ease. It seems sensible that if we have a gut knot, a feeling of tenseness in our gut, we are cutting off the flow of vitality from our gut that we depend upon for health and well-being.

A patient of ours once told us that she had a wise doctor who had said to her that "if your eyes can not cry, then your gut will". He was describing the reason your gut might be in pain physically in relation to emotional pain when your head brain is in denial. Your head and even your heart may be in denial, but your gut can't be. That you can count on! Have we not all had the experience of laughing or crying until our gut feels it. But if our thinking brain and our heart are in denial of our feelings and needs as Human beings, our gut will cry or signal us (i.e. irritable bowel syndrome, stomach pains, dis-ease, etc) like a red flag to be aware of ourselves and our instinctual Human needs of freedom and acceptance until our thinking brain gets the message.

The problem comes for most of us in that we don't always understand what our gut feeling is saying to us. Often, the gut is registering an impact of an experience from long ago that is being triggered in the present moment and our gut has stored the feeling memory of an unresolved issue. Our body image (how we think about our living body) is set in our memory from past events in our lives and therefore body sensation is a key to healing trauma and recalibrating our body maps, feeling ourselves from the inside out. We certainly are better off to explore our memories, by way of our gut feelings and bring some new light on the issue from the past that needs to be resolved, then move forward with our lives with a blind spot.

187

We have found that the Somatic Reflection Process on gut feelings is vital for improving the emotional immune system and mental health, as well as developing gut feeling awareness to follow in healthy decision-making. We recommend its use daily along with any probiotic diet plan to work hand-in-hand for gut disease and for general wellness. Make your gut happy with both good bacteria and gut feeling awareness to send the maximum signals of happiness to the thinking brain.

As you begin using the protocol for the Somatic Reflection Process, you will see that we started from the gut in our exploration of intelligence rather than from the head, a bottom-up approach to counseling and healing, and found the gut feeling memory to hold the record of the impact of life upon the person. We found that the awareness of this impact through gut or somatic reflection is the key to positive development and both physical and mental health and well-being. In fact, we have theorized that just as the body repairs cells during deep sleep, the Somatic Reflection Process—centering on gut feelings—has the same cell repair possibility as REM sleep or at the least enhances this process to occur. Our research in 2005 at Sonoma State University found that participants—a small sample with whom we used the Somatic Reflection Process—reported sleeping better after the process, felt less stress that reduced the gut knot feeling, and experienced a renewed clarity of thought, hope, decision-making, and somatic awareness.

Perhaps one of the most important ways that we can boost our immune system is to become aware of our gut feelings and reflect upon them to open the communication between the gut brain and head brain and give us a clear focus on our needs as Human beings. We have seen that in improving the gut-head

188

connection with the Somatic Reflection Process, there is a reduction of stress in the individual and this is the key to optimal health and wellness.

Researchers who are studying the head-gut connection and the affect of the gut on childhood development and on both mental and physical health, must look at the psychological needs that our gut feelings monitor. We feel certain that this approach will collaborate with a combination of medical and psychological approaches to gut health.

Many people are becoming painfully aware that we as a Humanity have gotten far away from the consciousness of our gut instincts and some people are afraid they will one day go away. We can assure you that this will not happen and that our gut instincts are alive and well, just a bit hidden in our unconscious. And they can be accessed and listened to by anyone with feeling reflection work. The question that is rarely explored in a specific way in books today is how to actually get in touch with these instincts.

The only way to truly understand what our gut instincts are is to reflect on the feelings in our gut and go back in time with our gut feeling reflection to an early childhood time when life was simple and our feelings were not so buried by our logic. When we do the work of this gut reflection, we find that our gut responses have always been there and hold the memory of the impact of experience upon us. As counselors, we have gone through this process with hundreds of people and no one, to our knowledge, has ever regretted the experience. Often times, the person was very willing to try this process because they were experiencing a gut knot or profound emptiness. But also, we used this method to deal with all adult problems in the here and now, including career confusion and decision-making,

189

relationship problems, personality and business problems, personal loss, grief, shame, returning vets, trauma, etc.

The gut instinctual feelings of emptiness and fullness—often confused with the feeling of empty and full in terms of the need for food—will always be concerned about the needs of the individual person for the balance of acceptance/connection and for control of one's own responses or the freedom to respond naturally. On the other hand, the thinking head may be working in behalf of everything and everyone else outside of us. It is worth noting here that we are not the only mental health educators that have discovered that the gut brain holds special keys to inner Human instinctual needs, functioning, and health; and that these needs help preserve our life and motivation to be who we are naturally. Over the recent years, methodologies from NLP (Neuro Linguistic Programming) have emerged to help hundreds of people align their head, heart, and gut brains for positive life decision-making and wellness.

In their revolutionary book published in 2012, *mBraining: Using your multiple brains to do cool stuff* (we know, we love their subtitle too), NLP practitioners Marvin Oka and Grant Soosalu conclude from their studies and highly successful clinical work with people all over the world that the gut brain (enteric nervous system) has prime functions related to what they call *core identity*, *mobilization*, and *self-preservation*. This is an exciting overlap in their work and in ours concerning the gut brain intelligence and functionality. (for more on Oka and Soosalu's work see mbraining.com)

It is easy to see the correlation between the first function that they name one's core identity (who we feel we are in essence) and in what we found to be named the gut feeling instinctual need for acceptance (to feel oneself to be accepted for who we feel that we are naturally).

The second of the two gut brain functions recognized by Oka and Soosalu, mobilization, relates to what we have called in our work 'the gut instinctual need to be in control of one's own responses to life' (the freedom to respond naturally). While there are some differences, both their and our terms— mobilization or control—may be viewed as a way to talk about the Human instinctual need to respond from within, without regard to the pressure from the external world around us, and to put into action/motion with the help of the logical brain our basic need to be free to do so.

The third function, as we see it, that Oka and Soosalu attribute to the gut brain, self-preservation, has some relationship to both of the two other functions in that the need for acceptance and control (or in Oka's and Soosalu's words, core identity and mobilization) are both instincts that allow us our important motivation for and self-preservation of life. We would say that when we are in balance and have both acceptance and control in our lives, we feel a sense of fullness in our guts that is an acknowledgement of our self-preservation and a state of balance.

Whatever words you choose to use, the functions of the gut responses relate to the deep understanding of being who we are naturally and are necessary to positive life decision-making and positive mental health. It is always inspiring when others in the field validate your scientific research and we expect much more validation to follow by others in the near future when there is more research on the intelligence of the gut brain.

In Summary

As we begin listening to the gut voice in our lives, the two brains—head and gut—begin to work together. This serves the individual and the community. Working to use our thinking head in consort with our gut brain and instinctual needs, brings our body-mind together, relieves stress, and opens the way of the heart, of the higher intuitive mind, and of wellness.

We have explored a new model of Human Nature with multiple brain intelligence—gut and head. With a greater awareness of our instincts and the uniting of head and gut, we have taken the first step towards increasing our Intuitional Intelligence. And with this greater intelligence, we have discussed the possible evolution of the Human species to be heading toward telepathy—which is just one example of what we may be capable of with the increase and emergence of our Human Intuitional Intelligence. We have also alluded to the idea that through higher Intuitional Intelligence we will guide our species into advanced scientific discoveries in tune with our inner nature, as we develop the instincts for even greater observation of Nature and Human Nature. We have advocated changes in our outdated educational system to include education of both the head and gut brains, in equal measures, and thus assist the young child through adulthood in understanding and developing awareness of his/her instinctual needs and feelings from moment-to-moment, in a student centered approach to learning. We have proposed the method of *Trail and Learn* and the development of the awareness of instincts rather than competition and failure as a dominant method of education. This would change our values as both individuals and societies, and it would make way for the development of beautiful creative minds. We have proposed

192

changes in our reliance on external religion and laws in favor of developing through education our awareness and the functional use of the self-regulatory system within us—our balanced and combined use of head and gut intelligence.

And perhaps most importantly, we have explored and presented more on the technique to unite body-mind through the Somatic Reflection Process on gut feelings and instinctual needs to increase feeling memory, enhance individual mental health and wellness, and to reduce stress caused from a lack of head-gut communication. With this lack of stress, there is a reduction of disease and an increase of longevity and life quality of elders. We see a future when humanity will have far less disease and self-regulate without the stress of having the head and gut in conflict. You may speculate many more possibilities for future Human Beings and cultures as we free the instincts, unite gut and head brain intelligence, and thus increase Intuitional Intelligence. We leave the rest of the puzzle for you the reader and your Intuitive Intelligence.

Bibliography and Resources for Further Reading

This Bibliography is provided to assist readers with deeper interests in the areas covered in this book. The references correspond to the subjects covered in this book about the gut brain as well as the psychology & functioning of this two brain system of intelligence. While many of the references were used in this book, we have also included additional material for further inquiry.

Abram, D. (1996). *The Spell of the Sensuous: Perception and language in a more than human world.* Vintage Books: New York, New York.

Bercik, P. et al. Microbiota and host determinants of behavioural phenotype in maternally separated mice. *Nature Communications* 6, Article number: 7735. (2015).

Bercik, P. *et al.* The anxiolytic effect of Bifidobacterium longum NCC3001 involves vagal pathways for gut-brain communication. *Neurogastroenterol. Motil.* 23, 1132–1139 (2011).

Blakeslee, S. and M. (2007) *The Body Has a Mind of Its Own: How body maps in your brain help you do (Almost) everything better.* New York: Random House Trade Paperbacks.

Blavatsky, H. P. (1931). *Isis Unveiled: Master-key to the mysteries of ancient and modern science and theology.* The Theosophy Company: Los Angeles, CA.

Campbell, J. (1991). *The Power of Myth.* New York, NY: Anchor.

Cawood, D. (2015). *The Secret Sabbatical.* Morgon Hill, CA: Bookstand Publishing.

Conger, J. P. (1988). *Jung and Reich: The body as shadow.* Berkeley, CA: North Atlantic Books.

Corbett, L. (1996). *The Religious Function of the Psyche.* New York: Routledge.

Damasio, A. (2012). *Self Comes to Mind: Constructing the conscious brain.* New York: Vintage.

Disque and Bitter *Journal of Individual Psychology*, in an article titled Emotion, experience, and early recollections: Exploring restorative reorientation processes in Adlerian therapy.

Eagleman, D. (2011). *Incognito: The secret lives of the brain.* New York, NY: Patheon.

Eliot, Lise, (1999). *What's going on in there? How the brain and mind develop in the first five years of life.* New York, NY: Bantam Books.

Farber, B., Brink, D., & Raskin, P. (1996). *The psychotherapy of Carl Rogers: Cases and commentary.* New York: Guilford Press.

Fox, M. (1999). *Sins of the spirit, blessings of the flesh.* New York, New York: Harmony Books.

Friedman, H.S. and Martin, L.R. (2012). *The Longevity Project: Surprising Discoveries for health and long life from the landmark eight-decade Ssudy.* New York, NY: Plume.

Gendlin, E. T. (1962). *Experiencing and the creation of meaning: A philosophical and psychological approach to the subjective.* Evanston, Illinois: Northwestern University Press:.

Gershon, M. (1999). *The Second Brain: A groundbreaking new understanding of nervous disorders of the stomach and intestines.* New York, NY: Harper Perennial.

Gigerenzer, G. (2008). *Gut feeling: The intelligence of the unconscious.* New York: Penguin Books.

Goleman, D. (2005) *Emotional Intelligence: Why it can matter more than IQ .* New York, NY: Bantam Books.

Goodman, P., Hefferlin, R.F., & Pearls, F. (1951). *Gestalt therapy: Excitement and growth in the human personality.* New York, New York: Dell Publishing Company, Inc.

Harris, J. (2001). *Jung and yoga: The psyche-body connection.* Toronto, Ontario: Inner City Books.

Henderson, J. L. (1964). Ancient Myths and modern man. In C. G. Jung (Ed.), *Man and his symbols* (pp.104-157). New York: Dell.

Henderson, J. L. (1967). *Thresholds of initiation.* Middletown, Connecticut: Wesleyan University Press.

Hillman, J. (1996). *The Soul's Code: In search of character and calling.* New York: Warner Books.

Holt, J. (1967). *How children learn.* New York: Pitman Publishing Corporation.

Holt, J. (1964). *How children fail.* New York: Pitman Publishing Corporation.

Jacobi, J. (1942/1973). *The Psychology of C.G. Jung.* Yale University Press: London.

Janoe, E. & Janoe, B. (1979). Dealing with feelings via real recollections. In H. A. Olson (Ed.), *Early recollections: Their use in diagnosis and psychotherapy.* Springfield, IL: Charles C. Thomas Publisher.

Jung, C. G. (1953). The archetypes of the collective unconscious. (2d ed.). (R.F.C. Hull, Trans.). In H. Read, M. Fordham, & G. Adler (Eds.), *Collected works of C. G. Jung* (Vol 7, pp 92- 104). New York, NY: Pantheon Books, Inc.. (Original work published in 1943)

Jung, C. G. (1959). Psychological types. In V. Laszlo (Ed.), *The basic writings of C. G. Jung.* (R. F. Hull, Trans.). New York: Random House. (Original work published 1938)

Jung, C. G. (1960a). Instinct and the unconscious. (R.F.C. Hull, Trans.). In H. Read, M. Fordham, & G. Adler (Eds.), *Collected works of C. G. Jung* (Vol 8, pp.129-138). New York, NY: Pantheon Books, Inc.. (Original work published in 1919)

Jung, C. G. (1961). *Memories, dreams, reflections.* (Winston, C. and Winston, R., Trans.). NY: Vintage Books.

Jung, C. G. (1969a). *Aion: Researches into the phenomenology of the self.* (R. F. Hull, Trans.). Princeton, NJ: Princeton University Press. (Original work published 1959)

Jung, C. G. (1969b). The concept of the collective unconscious. (R.F.C. Hull, Trans.). In H. Read, M. Fordham, & G. Adler (Eds.), *Collected works of C. G. Jung* (Vol 9, pp. 42-53). New York, NY: Pantheon Books, Inc.. (Original work published in 1936)

Jung, C. G. (1969d). Conscious, unconscious, and individuation. (R.F.C. Hull, Trans.). In H. Read, M. Fordham, & G. Adler (Eds.), *Collected works of C. G. Jung* (Vol 9, pp. 275-289). New York, NY: Pantheon Books, Inc.. (Original work published in 1939)

Kohut, H. (1977). *The Restoration of the Self.* New York: International Universities Press. Lao Tsu, (1972). *Tao Te Ching.* (G. Feng & J. English, Trans.) New York, NY: Vintage Books. (Original work published in 6th century B. C.)

Krystal, S. (2003). A nondual approach to EMDR: Psychotherapy as satsang. In J. Prendergast, P. Fenner, & S. Krystal, (Eds.). *The sacred mirror: Nondual wisdom and psychotherapy (pp. 116-137).* St. Paul, Minnesota: Paragon House.

Laird, J. & Bresler, C. (1990). William James and the mechanisms of emotional experience. *Personality and Social Psychology Bulletin,* 16(4), pp. 636-651.

Larsen, S. (1976). *The Shaman's Doorway.* New York, NY: Harper & Row.

Lefcourt, H. M. (1973). The Function of the Illusions of Control and Freedom. *American Psychologist, 28,* 417-426.

Li, M., Xue, X., Shao, S., Shao, F. & Wang, W. Cognitive, emotional and neurochemical effects of repeated maternal separation in adolescent rats. *Brain Res.* 1518, 82–90 (2013).

Levine, P. A. (1997). *Waking the Tiger: Healing trauma.* Berkeley, CA: North Atlantic Books.

Lieberman, M. (2014). *Social: Why our brains are wired to connect.* New York: Broadway Books.

Love, S. (2007). Using Somatic Awareness as a Guide for Making Healthy Life Choices. *Somatics Magazine-Journal Of The Mind/Body Arts and Sciences,* Volume XV, Number 2. (Silver Love is same person as author Martha C. Love)

Love, S. (2008). Healing the Trauma of the Body/Mind Split Through Accessing Instinctual Gut Feelings: A protocol for facilitating the somatic reflection process (SRP). *Somatics Magazine-Journal of The Mind/Body Arts and Sciences,* Volume XV, Number 4. (Silver Love is same person as author Martha C. Love)

Love, M.C. and Sterling, R.W. (2011). *What's Behind Your Belly Button? A Psychological perspective of the intelligence of human nature and gut instinct.* Charleston, SC.

Myers, I. B. (1962). *The Myers-Briggs Type Indicator: Manual 1962.* Princeton, NJ: Educational Testing Services.

Myers, I. B. (1980). *Gifts Differing*. Palo Alto, CA: Consulting Psychologist Press.

Oka, M. and Soosalu, G. (2012). *mBraining: Using your multiple brains to do cool stuff*. Lexington. KY.

Parnia, S. (2013). *Erasing Death: The science that is rewriting the boundaries between life & death*. New York, NY: Harper Collins Publishers.

Perls, F. (1969). *Gestalt therapy verbatim*. Lafayette, California,: The real People Press

Perera, S. (1981). *Descent to the goddess*. Toronto: Inner City Press.

Ralston, Peter. (2015). *Pursuing Consciousness: The book of enlightenment and transformation*. Berkeley, CA: North Atlantic Books.

Ramachandran, V.S. (2011). *The Tell-Tale Brain: A neuroscientist's quest for what makes us human*. New York, NY: W.W. Norton & Company.

Reich, W. (1961). *Selected writings*. New York: Farrar, Straus & Giroux.

Rogers, C. (1961). *On Becoming a Person: A therapist's view of psychotherapy*. Boston: Houghton Mifflin.

Shepherd, P. (2010) *New Self, New World: Recovering our senses in the twenty-first century*. Berkeley, CA. North Atlantic Books.

St. Clair, M. (2004). *Object Relations and Self Psychology: An introduction*. Belmont, CA: Brooks/Cole.

Van der Kolk, B. A. (2014). *The Body Keeps the Score: Brain, mind, and body in the healing of trauma*. New York, NY: Viking.

Winnicott, D. W. (1965a). The theory of the parent-infant relationship. In *The matura tional processes and the facilitating environment* (p. 37-55). New York: International Universities Press. (Original work published 1963)

Winnicott, D. W. (1965b). From dependence to independence in the development of the individual. In *The maturational process and the facilitating environment* (pp. 83-99). New York: International Universities Press. (Original work published 1963)

Winnicott, D. W. (1971). *Playing and Reality*. New York: Penguin Books.

Wittine, B. (1993). Assumptions of Transpersonal Psychotherapy. In R. Walsh & F. Vaughan, (Eds.). *Paths beyond ego: The transpersonal vision (pp. 165-170)*. New York: Jeremy P. Tarcher/Putnam.

Wood, J. D. (2011). *Enteric Nervous System: The brain-in-the-gut (Integrated Systems Physiology: From Molecule to Function to)*. University of Mississippi: Morgan & Claypool Life Sciences.

Woodman, M. (1982). *Addiction to Perfection*. Inner City Books: Toronto, Canada.

Woodman, M. & Mellick, J. (2000). *Coming Home to Myself: Reflections for nurturing a woman''s body and soul*. Boston, MA: Conai Press. Yogananda, P. (1983). *Songs of the soul*. L.A., CA: International Publications Council of Self-Realization Fellowship.

About the Authors

The Genesis of this book, *Increasing Intuitional Intelligence*, and it's companion, *What's Behind Your Belly Button?*, is based on the experience of the two authors working together in a college setting. Martha Char Love worked from 1970 until 1980 as a school psychologist/teacher/counselor and Bob (Robert) Sterling worked from 1967 until 1983, as an administrative educator/teacher/counselor. He had previous experience as an Electrical Engineer with experience in Industry and also held a theology degree from Duke University.

The cultural backgrounds of Martha and Bob proved to be salient aspects of the breadth of understanding of Human Nature that they had and were able to achieve in their work. Martha was born in 1947 and raised in the South. Bob was born in 1919 and raised in a Northern Ohio village. By the time of puberty, both had been affected by major traumas. Martha had contracted polio as a child and experienced the struggle to overcome the challenges of that debilitating illness. Bob was born at the end of the First World War and the beginning of the Great Depression with the loss of the family home, was moved to an undesirable neighborhood, and experienced extreme poverty at age thirteen. As an adult, Bob experienced a crippling event to his eldest child at age 5—which has raised many questions throughout Bob's adult life. In their work together, these challenges in their early lives became useful explorations of inner feeling experiences upon which to examine Human needs and gut responses.

Martha had experienced the impact of growing up in the South in the 50s and early 60s, and came equipped with a degree in Elementary Education and a Master's degree in Educational Psychology, with a license in School Psychology. Bob was carrying the direct impact of WWII in Europe, with an Electrical Engineering Degree, a Masters in Religious Education, and twelve years of industrial experience in Electronics.

While working as colleagues together at Santa Fe Community College in Gainesville, Florida, in the 1970s, they accepted the task of teaching and operating a Carrier Guidance and Assessment Program (Career Gap) that served both the community college students and as a use for the general public. The assignment was to establish a career center that would furnish students information about appropriate careers that they might choose for themselves based on personality, interests, experience, educational preparation, and goals. Personal counseling was available when requested.

Experience with groups and individuals soon allowed feelings of the students involved in the career center to surface at a variety of levels, which were centered on personal disturbances. Hours of study of what they were learning from students, suggested that the two counselors were tapping into genuine universal instinctive feeling intelligence, primarily focused in the gut area of the body. It was at that time that they first wrote a text for their classes about the gut instinctive responses that they were discovering with people they were working with in career exploration. They also during this time, developed the Somatic Reflection Process (SRP) on gut feelings to unite body-mind and used it with hundreds of people in the counseling therapeutic process.

The convergence of the two personalities and experiences, and the reflection on hundreds of other's personal traumas in counseling using the SRP, enabled them to critically look at what was happening in counseling methodology and medical discovery, particularly when dealing with a wide variety of personal and social problems of others. It is with these initial personal backgrounds and individual experiences, along with their own further clinical research on the Somatic Reflection Process, that led them through time to a more accurate, more satisfying, and a more stress free image of Human Nature.

Since their years of work together, both have continued to work and study in the field of psychology and education, as well as to keep up a correspondence comparing notes on their subsequent work in education. In 2005, Martha received her second MA in Depth Psychology and continued her study of the gut instinctive response in a research study at Sonoma State University. Bob continued to work in the educational field as a counselor and college teacher and then as an administrator in a privately funded experimental high school near Gainesville, Florida.

After years of study and new medical breakthroughs supporting the intelligence of the gut brain, in 2011 Martha and Bob published a groundbreaking book on their life work and introduced a new Gut Psychology in *What's Behind Your Belly Button? A Psychological Perspective of the Intelligence of Human Nature and Gut Instinct*. The present book, *Increasing Intuitional Intelligence: How the Awareness of Instinctual Gut Feelings Fosters Human Learning, Intuition, and Longevity* is written as a companion to their first book and further explores the importance of developing the consciousness of Human gut instincts as we learn and age throughout life.

Made in United States
Troutdale, OR
06/25/2023

10786805R00120